MW01601985

PRESENTED TO

-------------------------

RECEIVED FROM

-------------------------

DATE

-------------------------

# Wisd🍎m
## from the
# Desk

***Teacher's Edition***

90 Days of Encouragement,
Faith & Insight for Teachers

VERNESTINE KENT LOMAX

**WISDOM FROM THE DESK:** 90 Days of Encouragement, Faith & Insight for Teachers

**The House of Lomax Publishing Company**
Email: info@thehouseoflomax.com

All Scripture quotations, unless otherwise noted, are taken from the **King James Version** (KJV) of the Bible. Public Domain.
Cover and interior design by Eshan (Fiverr) Editor: Anita Minniefield
Book Design by JBooksDesigns of Fiverr
Producer: Carrol "Palmo" Paryo, CRMGCESTOSRIVER Music Group

Special thanks to my family, friends and prayer partners for their encouragement, support and love throughout this project. I would like to extend a very special thanks to Latia Ashley, who without knowing me personally, followed the leading of Holy Spirit and introduced me to the producer of this audio book. Your obedience opened a divine connection that only God could orchestrate. Thank you for hearing His voice and responding in faith. Because of your obedience, this message will now reach many hearts around the world.

Printed in the United States of America
**ISBN (Paperback): 979-8-9992211-2-4**
**ISBN (eBook): 979-8-9992211-3-1**

First Edition: November 2025
Published by **The House of Lomax Publishing Company**
Powder Springs, Georgia

This devotion is a work of testimony and inspiration. Names, details, and events have been shared with integrity and prayer, reflecting the real-life story of the author and God's divine orchestration.

# TABLE OF CONTENTS

### SECTION 1: CALLING & IDENTITY

### SECTION 2: HEART WORK & CHARACTER

## SECTION 3: CLASSROOM CULTURE

## SECTION 4: STUDENT CARE & RELATIONSHIPS

## SECTION 5: INSTRUCTION & ASSESSMENT

## SECTION 6: BEHAVIOR & RESTORATION

## SECTION 7: RESILENCE & RENEWAL

## SECTION 8: PARTNERSHIP & COMMUNITY

## SECTION 9: MILESTONES & MOMENTS

# DEDICATION

To God—the Creator of every classroom, every student, every lesson plan, and every teacher—this devotional is for You. It begins and ends with Your inspiration. Master Teacher, it is by Your divine design that I was called to teach, to lead, and to pour into others. Your wisdom shapes my lessons. Your presence guides my steps. Your love fuels my passion. I dedicate this book to You with a heart full of gratitude.

To my first teachers—my beloved parents who have received their wings—Professors Mom and Dad, the late Reverend James Thomas Kent and Mother Mary Deans Kent: Thank you for speaking destiny over me long before I ever stepped into a classroom. Daddy, thank you for recognizing and activating the teacher in me from the moment I was born by prophetically speaking, "Baby I want you to grow up and be a schoolteacher." Mama, your words, "Baby, always put God first, and you will make it," has carried me through every chapter of my life. Your legacy still lives on in every lesson I teach and every life I touch

To my first teaching experience, my most precious student, Jasmine. You were the first student God placed in my heart. Before I ever stood behind a desk, I was learning through you. Thank you for allowing me to grow, to love, and to discover the calling within me. You made me a teacher long before the title ever did. And for that, I'll always be grateful. To my husband, James Edward Lomax, thank you for continuing to journey with me into the ever-unfolding classroom of life. Your love, marked by patience, wisdom, and faith, inspires me daily. You remind me that learning never ends and that when love is rooted in God, it becomes the greatest lesson of all. I'm grateful to walk this path with you, my partner in purpose, my steady encourager, and my answered prayer.

To my very first classroom, my 13 siblings, Willie, Katrew, Thomas, Sally, William, Reversa, Charles, Danny, Glenwood, Nelson, Phyllis, Teresa, and Cathy. Each of you represents a chapter of love, laughter, and legacy in my life.

To those who are not longer with us. May you rest in peace —Sally, William, Charles, and Danny. Your light continues to shine through our memories.

To those who remain, thank you for teaching me about unique abilities, diverse personalities, and the many ways people learn. You were my first students, my first teachers, and my first lesson in the power of connection. And to every educator who shows up with courage, heart, and faith—This *WISDOM FROM THE DESK* is for you. May your classroom be filled with peace, may your spirit be sustained by prayer, and may your calling be strengthened daily by the One who called you. I dedicate this book to those who teach not just with words, but with love.

Keep showing up. Keep planting seeds. Keep inviting Him in... and receive your *WISDOM FROM THE DESK*.

# FOREWORD

My story with this book began before I ever entered a classroom. I was born two days before my mom was named North Carolina Teacher of the Year in 1995–1996.

As an only child, I had a front-row seat to see what great teaching really looks like: learning every name before the first day, rewriting a lesson at midnight because it hadn't landed, making room for every learner at the table. Our dining room was often a workshop of chart paper, sticky notes, and stacks of books. Excellence in our home wasn't occasional, it was daily, and it was love.

While visiting her classroom after school, I saw my mom spend additional time with students of every background and ability. She honored each child's strengths, scaffolded courage where it was needed, and raised the bar for those ready to stretch. Her guiding principle was simple: see the person first, then teach the content. Yes, she taught mathematics, but she also taught perseverance, empathy, and hope.

I was her first student. From the kitchen counter turned number line to late-night thesis revisions, her classroom tools became my life tools: clarity, structure, reflection, and persistence. She never did the work for me, but she always equipped me to do it myself. That is what you will find in *Wisdom from the Desk*. It is not theory alone, nor slogans. It is the distilled craft of a teacher who poured the same energy into her students as she did into raising a daughter to think, write, and lead. Page after page, you'll hear her voice: practical, compassionate, and grounded in faith.

If you are a teacher, I hope this book feels like a steady hand on your shoulder. May it remind you why you started, guide you through hard days, and give you fresh ways to center on what matters most: every child is gifted and capable of growth.

If you are a leader, parent, or student, these pages will make you feel seen and capable too. You'll discover the art of feedback without shame, rigor with warmth, and the kind of excellence that lifts everyone higher.

People sometimes ask me how I became who I am. The short answer is simple: I was raised by a teacher whose love looked like early mornings, late nights, hard questions, and constant belief. She showed me that intelligence grows when challenged, compassion is a discipline, and hope is something you practice.

This foreword is also a thank-you note to my mom. The woman who showed me what it means to steward a calling and to keep learning alongside those around you. May her wisdom inspire you as it has inspired me.

— Jasmine "Jas"

# INTRODUCTION

Before I was an author, I was a teacher—entrusted with shaping minds, guiding hearts, and planting seeds of purpose. I know the joy, the weight, and the weariness that come with this calling.

**WISDOM FROM THE DESK:** 90 Days of Encouragement, Faith & Insight for Teachers was created as a daily pause—a space to breathe, reflect, and remember God is with you. He hears every unspoken prayer and honors every effort poured out in love.

These 90 days create a rhythm that can carry you through the school year twice. The first time, you will find encouragement for the moment. The second time, you'll return with a fresh perspective and renewed faith.

Through this journey, may you discover strength for today, peace for tomorrow, and the assurance that your work matters, eternally. To every educator who rises early, stays late, and gives their all, my prayer is that you feel seen, strengthened, and inspired.

This is more than a book; it is an invitation to love your calling, even on the hardest days and deepen your commitment to students, family, colleagues, and yourself.

Remember, true wisdom and learning begin in the presence of God.

# ABOUT THE AUTHOR

**Vernestine Kent Lomax** is a retired, award-winning teacher, ordained elder, and author whose life has been marked by a deep love for students, educators, and the power of faith. Over decades in the classroom, she became known for her compassionate guidance, unwavering excellence, and unshakable commitment to teaching as both a profession and a calling.

She was named **North Carolina Teacher of the Year (1995–1996)**, representing over 75,000 educators statewide, was later honored among the Top 50 Teachers in the Nation, and was personally recognized by **President Bill Clinton**. Her contributions were further celebrated with the **Order of the Long Leaf Pine,** North Carolina's highest civilian honor, bestowed by Governor James Hunt. Her legacy is permanently enshrined in the **Nexus T. Freeman African American Museum**, where her story continues to inspire.

Beginning her career as a mathematics teacher, Vernestine went on to hold impactful leadership roles, equipping both students and fellow educators with wisdom, grace, and skill.

She holds a **Lifetime Teaching License** from the State of North Carolina, testament to her enduring impact. The secret to her success was spoken prophetically over her at birth by her parents and still guides her today as a teacher and servant leader: #GodFirstTeacher.

Today, Vernestine continues her influence as **founder of Regal Consultation, LLC** and **co-founder of The House of Lomax Publishing and Consulting Company**, providing strategic consulting, mentorship, and inspiration for educators, leaders, and faith-based communities. She is also the visionary behind the **Seniors of Success Program** (established in 2015), mentoring at-risk and graduating seniors toward brighter futures.

Through devotionals, mentorship, and faith-filled writing, she remains a guiding voice for educators everywhere. *Wisdom from the Desk: 90 Days of Encouragement, Faith, and Practical Insight for Every Teacher* is her heartfelt gift; an offering of rest, renewal, and inspiration to teachers who give their all every single day.

Vernestine is married to **James Edward Lomax**. Together, they share a blended family of three daughters: Jas, Hannah (Moses), and Katherine; and two treasured grandsons, Malachi and Maverick. They reside in **Powder Springs, Georgia**, where she continues to write, lead, and inspire with grace.

# HOW TO USE THIS DEVOTIONAL

*WISDOM FROM THE DESK* is designed as a daily pause to breathe, reflect, and be renewed. Each entry follows the same rhythm:

**Scripture:** Begin with a verse to anchor your heart. Read it slowly. Let it set the tone for your day.

**A Teachable Moment:** A short reflection connecting truth to the classroom—bringing wisdom, encouragement, and insight into your calling as an educator.

**Prayer:** A prayer to steady your spirit. Whisper it, declare it, or make it personal.

**Action Step:** A small but intentional practice to carry the lesson into your classroom, relationships, and daily life.

**Reflections:** Take a moment to pause. Journal, breathe, and listen for God's whisper. Don't rush into it.

## Helpful Tips

- Start or end your day with one entry.
- Reflections, prayers, and progress.
- Pray aloud, let your classroom become sacred ground.
- Revisit entries for fresh encouragement.

Wherever you teach, in a classroom, office, or online, this devotional is your reminder that when your work is rooted in prayer, God builds something unshakable in you.

# SECTION 1

. . . . . . . . . . . . .

## CALLING
## &
## IDENTITY

SECTION 1

# DAY 1

# FOUNDATION

## SCRIPTURE

*"Trust in the Lord with all thine heart; and lean not unto thine own understanding. In all thy ways acknowledge him, and he shall direct thy paths"*

**(PROVERBS 3:5-6)**

## A TEACHABLE MOMENT

Before the students arrive ... before the bell rings ... before the day begins, I kneel. I ask God to go before me to soften hearts, to guide my words, and to protect my peace. Prayer is my first step; it is my foundation.

When the classroom feels like a battlefield, prayer reminds me I am not alone. When I do not have the answers, prayer connects me to the One who does. This classroom is not just where I teach. It is where I minister. And every moment becomes sacred when it is built on prayer.

Today, teachers, I invite you to start here, on the foundation, *on your knees*. Because the only way to carry this assignment well is to invite Him in first and let Him take it from there. If you have never kneeled before teaching your class, try it once and watch how God takes the ordinary moments of your day and turns them into blessings.

## PRAYER

Heavenly Father, before I teach a lesson, I come to You to guide my thoughts and calm my spirit. Build this day on Your foundation and Your strength. In Jesus' name, Amen.

## ACTION STEP

Find a quiet moment before school begins. Lay your lesson plans on the foundation at the feet of Jesus. Ask Him to teach through you.

*Take a deep breath. Picture your classroom filled with God's peace and purpose then walk in, knowing He's already there.*

## REFLECTIONS

Pause here and write what He is whispering as you reflect on the foundation you're building in faith and in your classroom.

_____

_____

_____

_____

_____

_____

_____

_____

_____

_____

_____

_____

_____

_____

_____

_____

_____

# DAY 2

# CALLING

## SCRIPTURE

*"You have not chosen me, but I have chosen you..."*
**(JOHN 15:16)**

## A TEACHABLE MOMENT

This is not just a job; it is a calling. If it were about the paycheck, I would have left long ago. But God called me to more: to teach character, not just content. To model faithfulness, not just facts. To see students, not just scores. Here, in my classroom, I fulfill my calling, and each moment is sacred.

Wonderful Teachers! God has called you to this incredible work! Every word you share, every lesson you craft, and each prayer you lift makes a lasting impact. You're planting seeds today that will blossom into tomorrow's leaders. Teach with the love of Christ in your heart, step boldly into the purpose He's placed before you, and let your light shine brightly for

His glory. Never forget teaching isn't just a job; it's your divine calling!

## PRAYER

Heavenly Father, thank You for calling me to this assignment. Remind me that I am making an impact. Even when it is hard, help me honor the position You have placed on my life. In Jesus' name, Amen.

## ACTION STEP

Take a moment to write down *why* you started teaching. Reflect on the calling behind the role.

*God does not just call the qualified. He qualifies the called and you are one of them.*

# REFLECTIONS

Use this space to write what God is confirming about your calling.

_____

_____

_____

_____

_____

_____

_____

_____

_____

_____

_____

_____

_____

_____

_____

_____

_____

# DAY 3

# LEGACY

## SCRIPTURE

*"A good man leaveth an inheritance*
*to his children's children..."*

**(PROVERBS 13:22)**

## A TEACHABLE MOMENT

Legacy is not about awards or applause. It is about what is planted deep enough to grow after I am gone. The way I speak to students today can resonate for decades. The kindness I show, the prayers I pray, the words I release, all of it becomes seed. I may never see the full harvest. But I trust God will water what I sow in faith.

Teachers, this is not just about teaching for today. It is about leaving a legacy for children's children and children's children's children and unborn children you may never see. Teaching is about leaving your signature on the earth.

It is not just a job. It is a divine assignment. A sacred trust. So today, lift your head, take a deep breath, and walk in purpose. You are not just teaching minds. You are shaping history.

## PRAYER

Heavenly Father, help me leave a legacy that points others to You. Let my life be a seed planted in classrooms, hearts, and generations I may never see. In Jesus' name, Amen.

## ACTION STEP

Write a declaration that you want your students or co- workers to remember you by ... leave a legacy.

*Your legacy is not what you leave to people;*
*it is what you leave in them.*

# REFLECTIONS

Take this moment to reflect on the legacy your words and actions are shaping.

_____

_____

_____

_____

_____

_____

_____

_____

_____

_____

_____

_____

_____

_____

_____

# DAY 4

# ETERNITY

### SCRIPTURE

*"But lay up for yourselves treasures in heaven..."*
### (MATTHEW 6:20)

## A TEACHABLE MOMENT

One day, the lesson plans will be packed away, the desks cleared, and the classroom lights will be dim. But the love I gave, the prayers I whispered, and the encouragement I spoke into my students. Those will never fade.

I may never see the manifestation, but I know the prayers I prayed in faith matter. Each day, I show up with purpose, teach with passion, and love with intention. And even when it feels unseen, I know heaven sees me.

Teachers, each day is an opportunity to impact a life forever. Thank you for showing up with grace, for teaching with purpose, and for loving with intention. You are not just shaping minds; you are modeling what success looks like. And we honor you.

## A TEACHER'S PRAYER

Heavenly Father, let my motives be pure, my heart be surrendered, and my work be pleasing to You. Thank You for the reward of serving You in the lives of others. In Jesus' name, Amen.

## ACTION STEP

Write a short note or prayer to your future self. Remind yourself that this work is bigger than you and worth every ounce of sacrifice.

*When eternity is the goal, even the smallest act of love becomes priceless.*

# REFLECTIONS

Pause and write down what eternity shifts in your perspective today.

_____

_____

_____

_____

_____

_____

_____

_____

_____

_____

_____

_____

_____

_____

_____

# DAY 5

# SENT

## SCRIPTURE

*"The steps of a good man are ordered by the Lord..."*
**(PSALM 37:23)**

## A TEACHABLE MOMENT

This classroom isn't just where I work; it's where I was *sent*. Heaven didn't make a mistake with my placement. God Himself appointed me for this room, this school, this season. Every student I greet, every lesson I prepare, every obstacle I face is woven into His divine strategy for their lives and mine.

When the days get heavy, I remind myself: this is not just a job, and these are not just students. I was sent here as a living answer to someone's prayer and someone's future.

Teachers, your presence is not ordinary. Your obedience is not wasted. Your assignment is not small. You are a carrier of light, hope, and truth in the exact place God appointed for you.

The soil you're sowing into may not show its fruit today, but it will in God's perfect time.

## PRAYER

Heavenly Father, anchor me in the truth that I was sent. Let my feet be firm and my heart be full. In Jesus' name, Amen

## ACTION STEP

Write this on a sticky note: "I am assigned. I am aligned. I am anointed." Place it where you'll see it daily.

*You didn't just walk in the door; you were released into your assignment.*

# REFLECTIONS

Reflect here on where God is sending you, even in the small daily assignments.

_____

_____

_____

_____

_____

_____

_____

_____

_____

_____

_____

_____

_____

_____

_____

# DAY 6

# DIVINE

## SCRIPTURE

*"A man's heart deviseth his way ... but the Lord directeth his steps."*

**(PROVERBS 16:9)**

## A TEACHABLE MOMENT

It was supposed to be a quick walk to the copier, but Heaven had other plans. Halfway down the hall, I crossed paths with a student whose eyes carried the weight of something unspoken. They didn't need a lecture, just a moment, a smile, a reminder that someone saw them. That wasn't a coincidence; that was a divine appointment.

These moments aren't distractions from the work; they *are* the work. Divine appointments often slip in between our plans, tucked into the spaces we didn't schedule. It's in those hallway pauses, lunch line conversations, and after-class check-ins that God lets us partner with Him in someone's breakthrough.

Teachers, never underestimate the holy weight of what feels like an interruption. Every step you take between the bells is an opportunity for Heaven to speak through you. You're not just walking hallways; you're walking in purpose.

## PRAYER

Heavenly Father, help me walk slowly enough to notice the divine assignments in my students You place in my path. Let me experience the greatest lessons being taught between the bells. In Jesus' name, Amen

## ACTION STEP

Be present in the hallways. Someone needs your smile, your listening ear, your presence.

*Sometimes your best teaching happens outside the classroom.*

# REFLECTIONS

Write about the *divine* purpose in your daily work.

_____

_____

_____

_____

_____

_____

_____

_____

_____

_____

_____

_____

_____

_____

_____

_____

# DAY 7

# I CHOOSE

### SCRIPTURE

*"Choose you this day whom ye will serve..."*
**(JOSHUA 24:15)**

## A TEACHABLE MOMENT

Teaching isn't just my job ... it's my choice. Every day, I choose to show up with a heart ready to pour out. Even on the hard days, I choose this calling because God chose me for it first.

My choice says to my students, "You're worth it." It tells them I'm here on purpose, not by accident. And when they know I'm choosing them daily, they learn the power of showing up even when it's not easy.

Teachers, your choice carries eternal weight. The day you stop seeing teaching as a burden and start embracing it as a divine appointment, your classroom becomes a place where purpose thrives.

## PRAYER

Heavenly Father, thank You for choosing me to teach. Help me say yes to this calling each day with love, purpose, and joy, no matter the challenges. In Jesus' name, Amen.

## ACTION STEP

Sit quietly and write down three reasons you still choose to teach. Now, thank God for each one.

*By choosing to teach, I hope your actions inspire them to learn.*

# REFLECTIONS

Pause and reflect: What life lesson will you *choose* to teach today?

_____

_____

_____

_____

_____

_____

_____

_____

_____

_____

_____

_____

_____

_____

_____

_____

_____

_____

# DAY 8

# FAITH

## SCRIPTURE

*"Be not deceived; God is not mocked: for whatsoever a man soweth, that shall he also reap."*

**(GALATIANS 6:7)**

## A TEACHABLE MOMENT

Every day, I show lessons, encouragement, correction, and love. Sometimes the soil looks hard, and I wonder if anything is growing. But faith says: keep sowing. The harvest may not be visible yet, but God has promised it will come.

Teaching involves daily demonstrations, affirmations, realignment, and praise. Even when the soil doesn't show signs of life. Faith says: keep planting anyway.

Your job is obedience; God's job is the harvest. And He never fails. Seeds sown in faith will bear fruit, sometimes in the most unexpected seasons. Teachers, sow with joy today and know the harvest is already in God's hands.

## PRAYER

Heavenly Father, help me sow in faith with expectation, not exhaustion. Remind me that You are Father of the harvest, and my labor in You is never wasted. In Jesus' name, Amen.

## ACTION STEP

Write down three seeds of faith you've planted this week ... words, prayers, or acts of kindness, and thank God for them.

*You were not forced;*
*you chose to show up in love.*

# REFLECTIONS

Now turn inward and note how *faith* guides your classroom and life.

# DAY 9

# GOOD STUFF

## SCRIPTURE

*"Every good gift and every perfect gift is from above..."*
**(JAMES 1:17)**

## A TEACHABLE MOMENT

That one phrase, "You've got some good stuff in you," can change everything for a student. I've seen it lift drooping shoulders, spark a smile, and bring light back into eyes that were losing hope. I say it often because I mean it: there is gold in every child, and it's my calling to speak to it until they see it for themselves.

Teachers, our job is more than correcting what's wrong, it's calling out what's right. A well-placed affirmation can water the seeds of identity and purpose in a way that discipline alone never will.

Parent-teachers, you hold the power to shape how your child sees themselves. Your words can either build confidence or chip away at it. Be generous with your affirmations, catch them doing something right, and name it out loud.

## PRAYER

Heavenly Father, let me uncover and affirm the treasure You placed in each student. In Jesus' name, Amen

## ACTION STEP

Write "You've got good stuff in you" on a sticky note for someone who needs a word of encouragement today.

*Call out the good and watch it rise.*

# REFLECTIONS

Take time to notice and record the *good stuff* God is doing.

_____

_____

_____

_____

_____

_____

_____

_____

_____

_____

_____

_____

_____

_____

_____

_____

_____

_____

_____

# SECTION 2

. . . . . . . . . . . . .

# HEART WORK & CHARACTER

SECTION 2

# DAY 10

# FINGERPRINTS

## SCRIPTURE

*"The works of his hands are verity and judgment..."*

**(PSALM 111:7)**

## A TEACHABLE MOMENT

From bulletin boards to breakthroughs, my fingerprints are everywhere not for recognition, but as a quiet offering of service. Every chart I hang, every paper I grade, every project I inspire carries my unseen imprint. Even when no one calls my name, the evidence of my faithfulness remains.

In God's Kingdom, the marks we leave are not about fame they are about faith. Every detail done with love is a fingerprint of His excellence left behind for someone else to see. And long after we are gone, those prints tell a story of a teacher who showed up with both hands and heart.

Teachers, your fingerprints are the silent testimony of a faithful servant who leaves them everywhere love can be found.

School Resource Officers, your role may be outside the classroom, but your impact is everywhere. Your patience in the hallway, your calm voice, and your watchful eye also leaves a fingerprint of safety and care on our school community.

## PRAYER

Heavenly Father, let everything I touch carry excellence and compassion. In Jesus' name, Amen.

## ACTION STEP

Take pride in one small task today and leave your fingerprint of strength.

*Your legacy is not just in lessons, it's in fingerprints.*

# REFLECTIONS

Reflect on the *fingerprints* you are leaving on hearts.

_____

_____

_____

_____

_____

_____

_____

_____

_____

_____

_____

_____

_____

_____

_____

_____

_____

_____

# DAY 11
# POWER

*"Death and life are in the power of the tongue..."*
**(PROVERBS 18:21)**

## A TEACHABLE MOMENT

I have seen how one encouraging word can shift a student's whole day. I have seen the other side too how a single careless comment can crack a child's spirit. As a teacher, my words carry weight. They can plant seeds of confidence or cast shadows of doubt.

That is why I ask God to anoint my mouth to help me speak life, even when I am tired, even when I am frustrated, I also ask Him to silence me when I do not need to say a word. I want my voice to echo the Father's love.

Because in every word, there is the power to heal . . . the power to build . . . the power to affirm or the power to destroy. Teachers, never underestimate the power of your voice.

Speak with intention. Speak with grace. Speak with love because a student's or a colleague's breakthrough may begin with your words.

## PRAYER

Heavenly Father, bridle my tongue today. Let my words build, not break. Give me the wisdom to speak life over my students, my colleagues, and over myself. In Jesus' name, Amen.

## ACTION STEP

Speak one life-giving word of encouragement today, let your words carry the power to lift someone's spirit.

*When you intentionally affirm someone today, it gives them strength.*

## REFLECTIONS

"Pause and write about where your true *power* comes from."

_____

_____

_____

_____

_____

_____

_____

_____

_____

_____

_____

_____

_____

_____

_____

_____

_____

# DAY 12

# TEACHER

## SCRIPTURE

*"A word fitly spoken is like apples of gold ..."*
**(PROVERBS 25:11)**

## A TEACHABLE MOMENT

I remember my teacher saying, "Your words have impact, use them wisely." Those words became my compass, guiding every correction soaked in compassion, every affirmation grounded in truth, and every lesson taught with eternity in mind.

Years from now, may your voice still echo in hearts you may never see again. You're not teaching for a test, you're teaching for a testimony. Keep speaking life, hope, and identity. Though your voice may fade from their ears, your impact will remain in their becoming.

Teachers, let your words build legacies, not just lessons. Teach today as if Heaven is listening and trust that what you say matters more than you'll ever know.

## PRAYER

Heavenly Father, let my words be tools that build, not weapons that wound. In Jesus' name, Amen

## ACTION STEP

Write down one life-giving phrase you'll commit to saying often in the life of a student.

*Your words become memory markers*
*... speak with purpose.*

# REFLECTIONS

Take a moment to reflect on what it means to be a *teacher*.

# DAY 13

# THE MIRROR

## SCRIPTURE

*"But we all, with unveiled face, beholding as in a mirror the glory of the Lord,..."*
**(2 CORINTHIANS 3:18)**

## A TEACHABLE MOMENT

Every day, I look into the eyes of my students and often, it's like holding up a mirror. I see glimpses of their stories, their fears, their dreams... and sometimes, I see a reflection of my own. The truth is, my students mirror me more than I realize. They respond to the tone I set, the grace I offer, and the belief I speak over them. But just as I see them, I must also see myself clearly.

What am I reflecting? Is it patience, hope, strength, compassion even on the days when I feel depleted? The mirror tells the story not just of who they are, but of who I'm becoming as I teach them.

Teachers, never forget: your students are watching, listening, and learning; not just from your lessons, but from your life. You are more than an educator; you are a living mirror. Stand tall, look into the mirror, and see what God sees: a difference-maker, a world-shaper, and a reflection of His heart. Keep going, the story you're telling is powerful.

## PRAYER

Heavenly Father, let my life reflect You clearly. Let what they see in me become a mirror of who they can be in Jesus' name, Amen.

## ACTION STEP

Stand before the mirror today and thank God for who He's making you. Then remind a student of who they're becoming.

*The mirror tells the story, but you help rewrite the ending.*

## REFLECTIONS

Look into *the mirror* and reflect on what God is shaping in you.

# DAY 14

# SPEAK

## SCRIPTURE

*Life and death is in the power of the tongue..."*
**(PROVERBS 18:21)**

## A TEACHABLE MOMENT

Every word I speak has weight. A single sentence can lift a discouraged student, calm a frustrated parent, or bring peace to a tense classroom. My words are tools capable of building or breaking, healing or harming. Today, I choose to speak life over my students, my coworkers, my leadership, and even myself. Because my voice holds the power to shape identities, restore confidence, and plant seeds that will bear fruit long after I'm gone.

Teachers, your words matter more than you know. In moments of correction and celebration, frustration and triumph, your voice becomes part of your students' internal narrative.

Speak life. Speak truth. Speak purpose. Because one encouraging word from you might be the sentence they remember for the rest of their lives.

## PRAYER

Heavenly Father, may the words I speak bring healing, not harm. Let my classroom be filled with language that builds in the lives of every student I teach. In Jesus' name, Amen.

## ACTION STEP

Speak an intentional word of encouragement to one student in each class today.

*Your voice may be the only one that speaks life to them today.*
*Make it count.*

# REFLECTIONS

Reflect on the words you *speak* and the life they carry.

_____

_____

_____

_____

_____

_____

_____

_____

_____

_____

_____

_____

_____

_____

_____

# DAY 15

# SMALL MOMENTS

## SCRIPTURE

*"For who hath despised the day of small things?"*
**(ZECHARIAH 4:10)**

## A TEACHABLE MOMENT

I used to think only the big, bold moments made the difference, the breakthrough lesson, the life-changing conversation, the proud graduation hug. But now, I see it differently. Sometimes it's the smile in the hallway, the gentle nod of encouragement, or the quiet "I believe in you" whispered in passing that changes everything. God is present in those small, often unnoticed moments. I don't rush past them anymore, I look for Him in them.

Teachers, the miracle is not always in the spotlight, it's often in the stillness. The quick hallway glance, the gentle tone, and the encouraging post-it note are acts of transformation. Teachers, every small act of kindness, every glance of compassion, and every quiet prayer over a student matters. God is using even the unnoticed moments to work miracles through you.

## PRAYER

Heavenly Father, help me see You in the small moments. Open my eyes to divine moments hidden in everyday details. In Jesus' name, Amen.

## ACTION STEP

Slow down and intentionally bless someone in a small way today.

*Small moments in the classroom often carry eternal weight.*

# REFLECTIONS

Take a moment to reflect on the small moments that matter most.

_____

_____

_____

_____

_____

_____

_____

_____

_____

_____

_____

_____

_____

_____

_____

_____

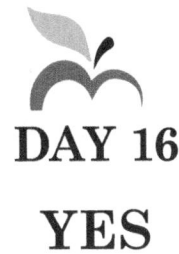

# DAY 16

# YES

### SCRIPTURE

*"Also I heard the voice of the Lord, saying, Whom shall I send... Then said I, Here am I; send me."*

**(ISAIAH 6:8)**

### A TEACHABLE MOMENT

My "yes" to God didn't just open a classroom it opened a calling. I said yes when it was inconvenient. I said yes when I didn't feel ready. I said yes without knowing the full story. And every time I said yes, God used it to write chapters in the lives of my students.

Yes, to show up when it was hard. Yes, to pray over names that others overlooked. Yes, to being a voice of encouragement when silence would have been easier. Each yes became a bridge that God used to reach hearts. Every yes encourages fellow teachers to keep going, assures parents their children are in good hands, and inspires administrators to keep investing in people over programs.

Teachers, your yes has weight in Heaven. It echoes into eternity. When you say yes to the moment, you may be unlocking a destiny whether in a staff meeting or a parent conference. The most powerful thing you can bring into the profession isn't a perfect plan, it's a surrendered yes.

## PRAYER

Heavenly Father, thank You for trusting me with this calling. Strengthen me to keep saying yes, even when it's hard. In Jesus' name, Amen

## ACTION STEP

Reaffirm your "yes" to God today. Say it aloud. Let it echo in your classroom.

*Your yes today could be the reason a student says yes to their purpose tomorrow.*

# REFLECTIONS

Reflect on the weight of your *yes* to God's calling.

# DAY 17

# IT'S TRUE

## SCRIPTURE

*"Sanctify them through thy truth: thy word is truth."*
**(JOHN 17:17)**

## A TEACHABLE MOMENT

When a student hears, "You are loved. You are chosen. You are enough," and quietly responds, "It's true," something powerful happens. Truth breaks through lies. It's the greatest gift we can give ... an identity anchored in God's Word.

When truth finally takes root, you'll hear them say, "It's true." That's the moment when your lessons, both academic and life, have moved from their ears to their hearts. Truth transforms. And when they discover it for themselves, it becomes unshakable.

Teachers keep planting truth, even when it feels unseen. One day, you'll see the fruit in their words and lives. One day, they will say, "It's true," and believe it.

## PRAYER

Heavenly Father, let every truth I speak spark healing and identity in my students. May they leave your presence in me, understanding who they are. In Jesus' name, Amen.

## ACTION STEP

Affirm a student today with truth that breaks shame.

*Truth does not lose its power just because it's questioned; it shines brighter every time it's lived out.*

# REFLECTIONS

Take time to write down the truths you know: *It's true.*

_____

_____

_____

_____

_____

_____

_____

_____

_____

_____

_____

_____

_____

_____

_____

_____

_____

_____

# DAY 18

# THEY SAY

## SCRIPTURE

*"Peter got down out of the boat, walked on the water and came toward Jesus."*

**(MATTHEW 14:29)**

## A TEACHABLE MOMENT

"They say you walk on water." I've heard it in the awe-filled voices of students who see something in me they can't quite explain. I smile, but I know the truth, if it looks like I walk on water, it's only because I've learned to walk by faith.

Teaching isn't about performing miracles in our own strength; it's about staying focused on the One who calls us out of the boat. Every lesson taught, every crisis calmed, every seed planted in the heart of a child happens because Christ is in me, steadying my steps.

Teachers, when admiration comes, let it point somewhere

greater. Let it lead to revelation, not of how gifted you are, but of the God who equips you. Our walk, like Peter's, only holds when our eyes are fixed on Jesus.

When students see patience that defies frustration, joy that outlasts hard days, or love that never runs dry, they're seeing the evidence of Christ in you. That's the true miracle.

## PRAYER

Heavenly Father, let every ounce of admiration I receive be redirected to You. Keep my eyes fixed on You, so my faith stays steady, and let my steps always lead my students to Your feet, in Jesus' name. Amen.

## ACTION STEP

The next time a student or parent praises you, respond with humility and a hint of testimony, acknowledge the compliment, but point them to the Source.

*They see your results, let them see your Source.*

# REFLECTIONS

Reflect on what *they say* and what God says about you.

_____

_____

_____

_____

_____

_____

_____

_____

_____

_____

_____

_____

_____

_____

_____

# DAY 19

# DON'T WASTE

## SCRIPTURE

*"Let this mind be in you, which was also in Christ Jesus."*
**(PHILIPPIANS 2:5)**

## A TEACHABLE MOMENT

We are surrounded by knowledge, books, degrees, certificates, professional development. But I've learned that having information isn't the same as walking in wisdom. The mind God gave us wasn't meant only for tests and titles it was designed to carry truth, create solutions, and reflect His glory.

Teachers, our role is not just to fill minds but to shape them for purpose. Challenge your students to think deeply, ask boldly, and grow purposefully. But also ask yourself how am I using my mind? Do I renew it daily with His Word? Do I anchor it in love, not pride? An unrenewed mind may be educated, but it will never be anointed.

Academic Coaches, your greatest lesson plan is not written on paper; it's written in the way you think. Let your mind be a living reflection of Christ's mind, and your influence will multiply far beyond the classroom.

## PRAYER

Heavenly Father, You've given me intelligence, opportunities, and training. Help me never to waste my mind on what doesn't matter. Let my thinking align with Your truth, and my teaching overflow with Your wisdom. In Jesus' name, Amen.

## ACTION STEP

Pause today and evaluate: What have I been thinking about most this week? Does it reflect purpose, faith, and growth?

*With all the education in the world, your mind should not be wasted.*

# REFLECTIONS

Consider how you will *not waste* your time, gifts, or influence.

_____

_____

_____

_____

_____

_____

_____

_____

_____

_____

_____

_____

_____

_____

_____

_____

_____

_____

# DAY 20

# WALK THE TALK

## SCRIPTURE

*"But be ye doers of the word, and not hearers only, deceiving your own selves."*

**(JAMES 1:22)**

## A TEACHABLE MOMENT

Students may not remember every fact you teach, but they never forget how you live. They are watching how you respond when stressed, how you speak about others, how you handle mistakes. Teaching isn't just instruction; it's demonstration. They notice when you stay calm under pressure, when you speak kindly in moments of frustration, and when you own your mistakes. Your walk will either validate your words or contradict them.

Teachers, integrity is when your actions reiterate your instruction. When you call for respect, you respond respectfully. When you expect accountability, you model it first. Sometimes the lesson they need most is not in the textbook, it's in the life they see before them.

## PRAYER

Heavenly Father, let my life be a lesson in love, grace, and integrity. Help me model the values I teach. And when I fall short, let even my apology teach humility. In Jesus' name, Amen.

## ACTION STEP

Identify one area this week where your actions and words can align more fully. Be intentional in walking it out in front of your students.

*What is God calling me to model more faithfully in front of those I teach?*

# REFLECTIONS

Pause and reflect on how you *walk the talk* each day.

_____

_____

_____

_____

_____

_____

_____

_____

_____

_____

_____

_____

_____

_____

_____

_____

_____

_____

# SECTION 3

· · · · · · · · · · · ·

CLASSROOM
CULTURE

# DAY 21

# NO COMPROMISE

## SCRIPTURE

*"But Daniel purposed in his heart that he would not defile himself..."*

**(DANIEL 1:8)**

## A TEACHABLE MOMENT

It's tempting to lower the standard to avoid conflict or fit in with a culture of mediocrity. But we are called to be thermostats, not thermometers, setting the temperature, not reflecting it. Excellence has a cost, and it's worth paying.

In a world that often lowers the bar to make things easier, teachers must stand for truth, fairness, and quality. Compromise may seem harmless in the moment, but it robs the future of its foundation.

Teachers, you are not called to blend in. You are called to stand out as a standard-setter, even when it's uncomfortable

Your commitment to excellence speaks volumes. Students notice when you hold the line, even quietly. Every time you stand for what's right, you teach courage without a single lecture. Your integrity is your legacy. Protect it at all costs.

Teachers, students don't just learn from your lessons, they learn from your standards. When you walk in integrity, you teach them courage without saying a word.

## PRAYER

Heavenly Father, strengthen my resolve when compromise feels easier. Help me stand for truth and excellence, even when it costs me comfort. In Jesus' name, Amen.

## ACTION STEP

Reflect on one area where you've felt pressure to lower your standard. Recommit it to God and take a stand today.

*Am I living by conviction or convenience in my classroom?*

# REFLECTIONS

Reflect on where you must stand firm with *no compromise.*

_____

_____

_____

_____

_____

_____

_____

_____

_____

_____

_____

_____

_____

_____

_____

_____

_____

_____

# DAY 22

# THE BELL

## SCRIPTURE

*"Cause me to hear thy lovingkindness in
the morning; For in thee do I trust."*

**(PSALM 143:8)**

## A TEACHABLE MOMENT

Before the bell rings, before the noise, before the questions, and
before the papers pile up, I need a moment. A moment with
God. A moment to let Him steady me before I stand before my
class. It does not have to be long. Just long enough for Him to
remind me: I am not alone.

I invite Him in while the room is still quiet, before the students arrive, and He meets me there. The bell may mark the
beginning of class, but it does not define the atmosphere. Prayer
does.

Teachers, your quiet moment with God sets the tone for the rest of your day. Keep inviting Him in, and He will show you the way. And if you've never made that space before, know this: any day you decide to open the door, He is already waiting. Give Him a chance ... and watch what happens after the bell rings.

## PRAYER

Heavenly Father, meet me in the quiet. Fill me before the bell rings. Prepare my heart so I can be a light and a source of strength to others. In Jesus' name, Amen.

## ACTION STEP

Arrive five minutes early tomorrow. Sit at your desk and whisper a prayer over your classroom.

*Before the bell rings, take a moment to
start your day in His stillness.*

## REFLECTIONS

Write about what happens for you and your students *beyond the bell.*

_____

_____

_____

_____

_____

_____

_____

_____

_____

_____

_____

_____

_____

_____

_____

_____

_____

_____

# DAY 23

# QUESTIONS

## SCRIPTURE

*"If any of you lacks wisdom, let him ask
God... and it shall be given to him."*

**(JAMES 1:5)**

## A TEACHABLE MOMENT

I've heard it countless times: "This might be a dumb question..."
But I know that in God's Kingdom, curiosity is not foolish it's
faith in motion. A raised hand is more than a request for information; it's an act of courage. In my classroom, asking questions
is never a weakness—it's worship.

And just as my students are learning to ask without fear,
so am I. When I don't know, I go to the Father. When I feel
stretched, I ask for strength. When the path is unclear, I ask for
wisdom because the God who invites questions is the same God
who releases revelation.

Teachers remember that every question is an open door. Sometimes the bravest thing a student will ever do is ask you for help, and the most powerful thing you can do is point them toward the One who never withholds answers.

## PRAYER

Heavenly Father, help me foster a classroom of courage to ask questions. Remind me that asking is not a weakness, it's worship. In Jesus' name, Amen

## ACTION STEP

Model vulnerability today. Ask your students a question you don't already know the answer to.

*The bravest hand in the room is the
one that rises with a question.*

# REFLECTIONS

Reflect on the *questions* that matter most in your teaching and your faith.

_____

_____

_____

_____

_____

_____

_____

_____

_____

_____

_____

_____

_____

_____

_____

_____

# DAY 24

# MORE THAN

## SCRIPTURE

*"And now abideth faith, hope, charity, these three; but the greatest of these is charity."*

**(1 CORINTHIANS 13:13)**

## A TEACHABLE MOMENT

My classroom is not simply a room, it's a sanctuary where faith is nurtured, hope is restored, and love is given without measure. Yes, I teach content. Yes, I grade papers. But I also listen to dreams, wipe tears, and believe in futures that my students can't yet see.

This room is my pulpit, my mission field, and my place of sowing. Every smile, every kind word, every prayer over a desk before the day starts, these are the invisible seeds that Heaven counts.

Teachers, never underestimate the power of your presence. Your love is not extra; it's essential. The greatest curriculum you carry is not written in a book; it's written in how you treat the people in front of you.

## PRAYER

Heavenly Father, fill my classroom with Your love. Let every student experience kindness, safety, and grace. More than a teacher, you are a living lesson in love. In Jesus' name, Amen

## ACTION STEP

Speak a word of love or affirmation over a student today, one who may need it most.

*Your greatest lesson may be the love you give.*

# REFLECTIONS

Take a moment to write how you are *more than* what others may see.

_____

_____

_____

_____

_____

_____

_____

_____

_____

_____

_____

_____

_____

_____

_____

_____

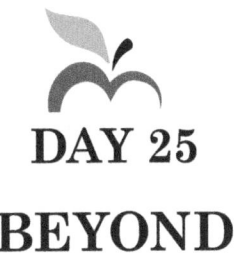

# DAY 25

# BEYOND

## SCRIPTURE

*"Be ye followers of me, even as I also am of Christ."*
**(1 CORINTHIANS 11:1)**

## A TEACHABLE MOMENT

The curriculum may tell me what to teach, but life gives me opportunities to teach beyond it. I didn't know they were watching when I stayed calm under pressure. I didn't know they were learning from how I forgave quickly or admitted when I was wrong. Yet these moments, unplanned and unscripted, become the lessons stay the longest.

Beyond the curriculum, my life is the living textbook. Every act of integrity becomes a chapter. Every moment of grace becomes a paragraph. Every time I choose patience over frustration, I am writing lines of hope on their hearts.

And when other voices, parents, coaches, administrators, echo those lessons, they sink even deeper.

Teachers, your greatest lessons are often caught, not taught. Your consistency is the lecture. Your compassion is an illustration. And your faithfulness is the final exam that leaves an eternal mark.

## PRAYER

Heavenly Father, let my life reflect You, even when I don't realize I'm being watched. Sometimes your best teaching is done by example, not instruction. Even when nothing is spoken, it helps me realize I'm still speaking volumes. In Jesus' name, Amen

## ACTION STEP

Write one thing you can model today, that maybe the reason someone keeps going **tomorrow.**

*The quiet lessons you teach may be the loudest ones they'll remember.*

# REFLECTIONS

Reflect on how your influence goes *beyond* the classroom walls.

# DAY 26

# I WANT

## SCRIPTURE

*"Let your light so shine before men..."*
## (MATTHEW 5:16)

## A TEACHABLE MOMENT

When a student says, "I want your class," I know it's not just the content, it's the climate. They're not only drawn to the lessons; they're drawn to the light. They're also drawn to peace. It's the peace they feel when they walk through the door, the way their voice matters, the safety they find in knowing they won't be shamed here.

Our classrooms can be living testimonies that the presence of God brings order, joy, and stability. The way we set the tone, the way we greet them, the way we handle conflict, these things create an atmosphere they want to be a part of.

Sometimes the greatest lesson you teach is the one you live out in the culture of your classroom.

When a student says, "I want your class," it's not just about the subject; it's about the space you create. They want a place where they feel safe, seen, and inspired.

Teachers, protect the climate of your classroom. It's not just where lessons happen, it's where hearts are healed.

## PRAYER

Heavenly Father, let my classroom reflect Your light and peace. May students long to be here not just to learn, but because they feel at home. In Jesus' name, Amen.

## ACTION STEP

Walk into your classroom today and intentionally speak peace over the space.

*Your classroom is more than a place; it's a safe haven.*

# REFLECTIONS

Write about what you truly *want* for your students and for yourself.

_____

_____

_____

_____

_____

_____

_____

_____

_____

_____

_____

_____

_____

_____

_____

_____

# SECTION 4

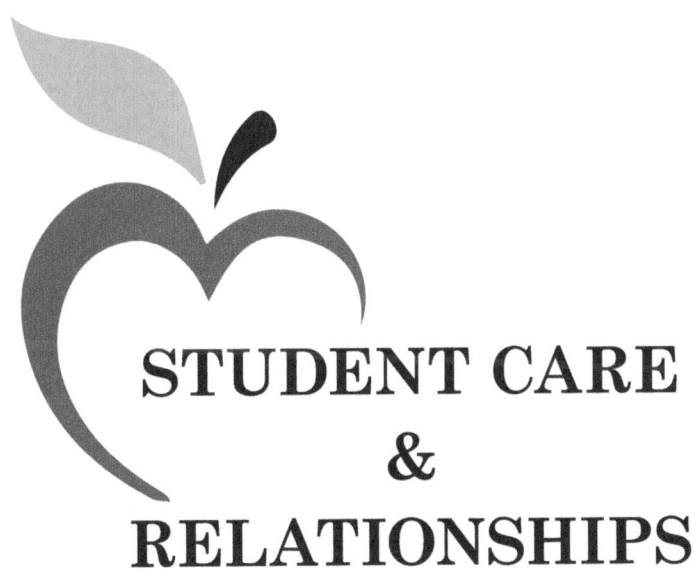

# STUDENT CARE
# &
# RELATIONSHIPS

# DAY 27

# REAL

### SCRIPTURE

*"Let love be without dissimulation..."*
**(ROMANS 12:9)**

### A TEACHABLE MOMENT

The greatest compliment I ever received came from a student who said, "That teacher is real." Realness is not about perfection; it's about consistency, humility, and sincerity. It's loving enough to admit mistakes and strong enough to live what you teach.

When students sense authenticity, they lower their walls. Trust grows. And once they trust you, your influence multiplies far beyond the lesson plan.

Teachers, authenticity is the bridge between teaching and transformation. Be real.

Librarians, your authenticity draws students in. When they see your genuine love for reading, research, and discovery, they know the library is more than a place, it's a safe haven for questions and creativity.

## PRAYER

Heavenly Father, help me to be real with grace, humility, and truth. Let my life be an honest witness. In Jesus' name, Amen.

## ACTION STEP

Share a moment of real struggle or growth with your students today where appropriate.

*When they believe it's true, you've done your real job*

## REFLECTIONS

Reflect on what it means to be *real* with your students and yourself.

_____

_____

_____

_____

_____

_____

_____

_____

_____

_____

_____

_____

_____

_____

_____

# DAY 28

# THEIR NAMES

## SCRIPTURE

*But now thus saith the Lord that created thee,*
*O Jacob, and he that formed thee,*
*O Israel, Fear not: for I have redeemed thee, I*
*have called thee by thy name; thou art mine.*

**(ISAIAH 43:1)**

## A TEACHABLE MOMENT

Every name on my roster matters. Each one is a soul with a story. Some stories I may never know, but God knows them all. So, I pray over the names of my students, one by one. This is not just a roll call; it is an opportunity to intercede.

God has entrusted these students to me, not just for mathematics but for moments of kindness and maybe even healing. Their names are not by accident, and neither are mine. I was chosen to be their teacher. I was chosen to be a positive presence in their lives. And so were you.

Teachers, your impact reaches beyond the lesson plan and beyond the year. Even when the fruit feels hidden, keep planting. Keep praying. God sees… and He's smiling.

## PRAYER

Heavenly Father, help me to see my students the way You do. Let their names remind me of their worth. Teach me to love them with Your heart. In Jesus' name, Amen.

## ACTION STEP

Take a few minutes today to speak blessings aloud over your student roster.

*They are not just students. They are sons and daughters of the King.*

# REFLECTIONS

Take a moment to reflect on how their names have influenced your life as a teacher.

_____

_____

_____

_____

_____

_____

_____

_____

_____

_____

_____

_____

_____

_____

_____

_____

_____

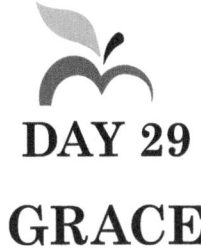

# DAY 29

# GRACE

## SCRIPTURE

*"But love ye your enemies, and do good..."*
**(LUKE 6:35)**

## A TEACHABLE MOMENT

Some students are easy to love. Others stretch me. Test me. But every child is someone's son or daughter and more than that, every child is someone made in God's image.

When I am tempted to react with frustration, I pray for grace. Grace to see the hurt behind the behavior. Grace to correct with compassion. Grace to model Christ, even when it is hard. Because they are not just here to learn, they are here to be loved.

Teachers, if you are navigating these challenges, never forget the sacredness of your role. You are the bridge between chaos and calm, correction and compassion, learning and love. When you lead with grace, you leave a legacy that reaches beyond the classroom. Keep loving but most importantly, keep talking to God.

## PRAYER

Heavenly Father, give me the grace and patience to deal with those who push boundaries. Help me see them through Your eyes. Use me to break cycles and build bridges, in Jesus' name, Amen.

## ACTION STEP

Pray for the student who challenges you most. Ask God for one new way to reach them today.

*Grace does not excuse behavior. It*
*transforms it from the inside out.*

## REFLECTIONS

Take time to write how you can extend *grace* in hard moments.

_____

_____

_____

_____

_____

_____

_____

_____

_____

_____

_____

_____

_____

_____

_____

_____

# DAY 30
# MINISTRY

## SCRIPTURE

*"God is our refuge and strength, a very
present help in trouble."*

**(PSALM 46:1)**

## A TEACHABLE MOMENT

Sometimes, it is not about what I teach, it is about being there.
Just showing up. Just listening. Just staying calm when everything feels chaotic. God's presence in my life reminds me—I
do not have to say a lot to make a difference. Sometimes, my
presence is the ministry. Sometimes, my presence is the lesson.
When I carry God's peace into the room, I create a space for
students to exhale. And in that space… healing begins.

Teachers, if you are wondering if the small moments matter,
know this: your quiet presence speaks louder than you think.
When you walk in peace, you shift the atmosphere. When you

remain rooted, you become a refuge. God is using your presence to make sacred space where hearts can breathe, believe, and begin again.

## PRAYER

Heavenly Father, help me carry Your presence wherever I go. Let my classroom be a safe place, a holy place, even when it looks like a mess. May I reflect You more than I reflect my stress. In Jesus name, Amen.

## ACTION STEP

Instead of fixing or advising today, be still and present with a student who simply needs your attention.

*You do not have to do everything.*
*Sometimes, your presence is the miracle.*

## REFLECTIONS

Reflect on how your teaching becomes *ministry* in everyday
ways.

_____

_____

_____

_____

_____

_____

_____

_____

_____

_____

_____

_____

_____

_____

_____

# DAY 31

# YOUR BACK

## SCRIPTURE

*"Bear ye one another's burdens and
so fulfil the law of Christ."*

**(GALATIANS 6:2)**

## A TEACHABLE MOMENT

In a world that gives up too easily, I look my students in the eye and say, "I've got your back." And I mean it. It's more than a phrase, it's a promise of safety, support, and consistency.

When students know I'm in their corner, they begin to take risks, believe in their potential, and push past limitations. To parents, it's a message of partnership: we're in this together. To colleagues, it's a commitment to unity we rise by lifting each other. Whether it's covering a class, sharing resources, or offering encouragement, we are better when we've got each other's back.

So, I chose to stay. I choose to dig deep. I show up when it's hard, speak life when it's heavy, and love fiercely even when it's not easy. One voice of consistency, one heart of compassion, one teacher who says, "I've got your back," can change everything. Teachers, can we count on you?

## PRAYER

Heavenly Father, help me be the kind of teacher who sees beyond the behavior and into the heart. Thank You for having my back so I can have theirs. In Jesus' name, Amen.

## ACTION STEP

Speak life into someone who may be carrying more than they're showing. Let them know: "You're not alone. I've got your back."

*Having their back does not mean you carry them; it means you cover them.*

## REFLECTIONS

Write about the importance of telling others, 'I've got *your back.*

_____

_____

_____

_____

_____

_____

_____

_____

_____

_____

_____

_____

_____

_____

_____

_____

# DAY 32

# THAT NAME

## SCRIPTURE

*"A wise man will hear, and will increase learning; and a man of understanding shall attain unto wise counsels;"*

**(PROVERBS 1:5)**

## A TEACHABLE MOMENT

The word "Teacher" is more than a title; it's a mantle. When a student calls me "Teacher," they're not just acknowledging my role, they're honoring my impact. That name tells the story of trust built, truth spoken, and lives shaped.

I wear it with humility because I know the weight it carries. To the world, it might be a job. To Heaven, it's a calling. And every time my name is spoken in that way, I am reminded: God trusted me with His children for this season. Teachers, you don't just have a title, you have a testimony.

The way you live, the way you love, the way you teach will give that name either weight or emptiness. Choose weight. Choose honor.

## PRAYER

Heavenly Father, thank You for the sacred title of "teacher." Help me wear it with humility, integrity, and love. In Jesus' name, Amen

## ACTION STEP

Write your name followed by the word *Teacher* on a sticky note. Place it where you can see it daily because that name carries divine weight.

*You don't just answer to "Teacher"; you rise into it.*

# REFLECTIONS

Reflect on the weight and honor of carrying the title *teacher.*

# DAY 33

# I BELIEVE

## SCRIPTURE

*"With men this is impossible; but with
God all things are possible."*
**(MATTHEW 19:26)**

## A TEACHABLE MOMENT

I've looked into eyes that have heard "you'll never be enough" more times than I can count. The enemy tries to plant doubt early, but my words can uproot it. When I look a student in the eye and say, "I believe in you," something shifts. They may not believe it yet, but my faith speaks to their future.

Belief is contagious. When they know I believe in them, they start to imagine that maybe, just maybe, God believes in them too. When that same belief is repeated by a counselor, a parent, a principal, or a coach, it becomes nearly unshakable. And that changes everything.

Teachers, your belief is a mirror reflecting their God-given worth. Sometimes it's not the lesson plan that changes them it's the unwavering certainty in your voice when you declare, "You can do this."

## PRAYER

Heavenly Father, let my words echo Your heart. Help me to speak faith even when results are slow. In Jesus' name, Amen

## ACTION STEP

Say "I believe in you" to a student today and follow it with why.

*When a teacher believes, a student rises.*

# REFLECTIONS

Write about the power of saying, *I believe in you.*

_____

_____

_____

_____

_____

_____

_____

_____

_____

_____

_____

_____

_____

_____

_____

_____

_____

_____

# DAY 34
# POTENTIAL

## SCRIPTURE

*"Man looketh on the outward appearance,
but the Lord looketh on the heart."*

**(1 SAMUEL 16:7)**

## A TEACHABLE MOMENT

When I say, "I see potential in you," I'm not complimenting their present; I'm prophesying their future. I'm calling forth the leader, the healer, the innovator that God already sees. Spotting potential is one thing; calling it out as a united team is another. When colleagues, administrators, and parents join in speaking life over a student, we create a chorus of encouragement that drowns out the noise of doubt.

Teachers, don't be distracted by the surface. Every roll of the eyes, every crossed arm, every missed assignment can't cancel what God has planted inside. Your words can water what's been buried. Keep speaking to what you see—not just with your eyes, but with your spirit.

## PRAYER

Heavenly Father, give me eyes to see my students the way You do, full of promise, full of purpose. Help me to not just manage behavior but awaken destiny. In Jesus' name, Amen

## ACTION STEP

Identify a student who's been overlooked and affirm their God-given potential today.

*Potential may be hidden, but it is never absent.*

# REFLECTIONS

Reflect on the hidden *potential* you see in your students.

# DAY 35

# THE LADY

## SCRIPTURE

*"Ye are the light of the world.*
*A city that is set on an hill cannot be hid."*
**(MATTHEW 5:14)**

## A TEACHABLE MOMENT

When students ask, "Where the lady at?" after I'm absent, I'm reminded that my presence matters. Even when they don't say it, they notice my consistency, my light, my influence. That question isn't just about location, it's about connection.

They may not remember my full name, but they remember the consistency of my presence. "Where the lady at?" means, "Where's the one who listens, cares, and shows up?"

Teachers, let them find you faithful. In a world full of instability, your reliability becomes a picture of God's steadfast love. Your consistent presence is your loudest lesson. It says, "I am here for you, no matter what." Even on days you feel unseen, you are anchoring hearts. Keep showing up because your presence is someone's peace.

## PRAYER

Heavenly Father, thank You that my presence carries peace and stability for my students. Help me to show up with intention, knowing You use even my consistency to minister. In Jesus' name, Amen.

## ACTION STEP

See your presence today as an opportunity, not an obligation.

*You are noticed more than you know.*

## REFLECTIONS

Write about how your consistent presence, 'the lady', impacts lives.

_____

_____

_____

_____

_____

_____

_____

_____

_____

_____

_____

_____

_____

_____

_____

_____

# DAY 36

# BURNING

## SCRIPTURE

*"He brought me up also out of an horrible pit... and established my goings."*

**(PSALM 40:2)**

## A TEACHABLE MOMENT

Not every rescue is dramatic. Sometimes it's as simple as noticing, listening, or speaking a kind word at the right moment.

When a student says, "You kept me from burning," they're telling you that your intervention, big or small saved them from a destructive path. You may never know the full weight of what you stopped, but Heaven does.

Teachers, your awareness is a shield. Stay prayerful. Stay attentive. Sometimes your quick word or act is the difference between despair and hope. Sometimes your faith becomes someone's fire escape, and you may never know how close to the edge they were.

## PRAYER

Heavenly Father, thank You for using my obedience to protect and rescue those who are silently struggling. Restore what has been poured out and refresh me for the days ahead. In Jesus' name, Amen.

## ACTION STEP

Speak life to a quiet student today. God may be using you to save them from unseen danger.

*They didn't burn because you stood in the gap.*

# REFLECTIONS

Reflect on how your awareness can keep a student from *burning* out.

_____

_____

_____

_____

_____

_____

_____

_____

_____

_____

_____

_____

_____

_____

_____

_____

# DAY 37

# FOR ME

## SCRIPTURE

*"Blessed are they which do hunger and thirst after righteousness: for they shall be filled."*
**(MATTHEW 5:6)**

## A TEACHABLE MOMENT

A student peeked in and asked, "You got something for me today?" It wasn't about paper; it was about hope. They expect something good... and I don't want to let them down. Some students walk in expecting correction or indifference. But when they start asking, "You got something for me today?" they're telling you they've come to expect life-giving words. It wasn't about paper; it was about hope. Your daily deposit of encouragement is like a spiritual and emotional breakfast; it fuels them for the day. They came expecting something good. I've learned that holy expectation is an open door for God to work through me.

Teachers, be ready. Have something uplifting in your mouth every day, because they're hungry for more than knowledge; they're hungry for hope. Every time we offer encouragement, spark curiosity, or discuss life, we are serving a meal that nourishes the spirit. Students will return to where they know they'll be fed. Be the kind of teacher whose "something" is worth coming back for every single day.

## PRAYER

Heavenly Father, let me always carry something worth giving a word, a smile, a seed of hope. May I be ready to feed every hunger You place in my path. In Jesus' name, Amen.

## ACTION STEP

Prepare one extra word of encouragement or resource for a student who's been searching.

*Yes, I got something for you today: love, truth, and hope.*

# REFLECTIONS

Write about the ways you can show students you have something *for them* to give.

_____

_____

_____

_____

_____

_____

_____

_____

_____

_____

_____

_____

_____

_____

_____

_____

_____

# DAY 38

# I KNOW

## SCRIPTURE

*"Honour thy father and thy mother..."*
**(EXODUS 20:12)**

## A TEACHABLE MOMENT

"I know your parents," can make a student stand a little taller or a little straighter. It's a reminder that character and legacy are connected. It's been my experience that when a student knows you really know their parents ... they shine a little brighter. Why? Relationship matters.

Building trust with families can open doors to deeper influence in the classroom. You're not just teaching a child, you're partnering with the people who love them most.

Teachers, knowing where they come from can help you guide where they're going. It's important to keep the family connection alive. When you honor their roots, you help them grow stronger branches.

## PRAYER

Heavenly Father, help me to see the whole picture of each student, past, present, and potential. In Jesus' name, Amen.

## ACTION STEP

Connect with one parent or guardian this week just to share something good.

*A teacher's words can reconcile generations.*

# REFLECTIONS

Reflect on the importance of saying, *I know your story matters.*

_____

_____

_____

_____

_____

_____

_____

_____

_____

_____

_____

_____

_____

_____

_____

_____

_____

# DAY 39

# PRESENCE

### SCRIPTURE

*"Let your light so shine before men..."*
**(MATTHEW 5:16A)**

## A TEACHABLE MOMENT

Sometimes I enter a room and peace follows. Not because of me but because of Who lives in me. Classrooms can carry tension, chaos, or even fear. But when a teacher walks in carrying the Spirit of God, the atmosphere realigns to Heaven's order.

Our presence is more than our body, it's the aroma of Christ filling a space. The smile we offer, the tone we carry, the stillness in our spirit, it all becomes a quiet announcement that peace is here.

Teachers, your presence can turn a storm into still waters; walk in knowing you carry the calm of Christ.

Teacher Assistants, you carry more than students—your presence carries peace, joy, and stability. The way you greet a child, handle a conflict, or offer a kind word shifts a rough morning into a hopeful day.

## PRAYER

Heavenly Father, shift the atmosphere through me. Let my presence carry Your peace. In Jesus' name, Amen.

## ACTION STEP

Walk your classroom before students arrive, pray in every corner, and watch His presence in you shift your day.

*You don't just manage space, you transform it.*

# REFLECTIONS

Reflect on how your *presence* changes the atmosphere.

# DAY 40

# YOU CAN

## SCRIPTURE

*"I can do all things through Christ
which strengtheneth me."*

**(PHILIPPIANS 4:13)**

## A TEACHABLE MOMENT

I've looked into the eyes of students on the verge of quitting and chosen to speak the opposite of their fear: "You can do it." These words aren't empty cheerleading; they are seeds of belief planted in soil that may be starved for hope.

Sometimes our faith in them becomes the scaffolding they lean on until they can stand in their own. In that moment, "You can do it" is more than encouragement; it's a prophecy over their potential.

Teachers, when you say, "You can do it," you are lending them your faith until they find their own.

Bus Drivers, your job requires skill, patience, and heart. On the hard days, remember you are modeling what "You can do it" looks like. It's more than driving a route. It's driving the first and last moments of a student's school day, and those moments matter.

## PRAYER

Heavenly Father, help me speak, "You can do it.", boldly into my students especially when they doubt themselves. In Jesus' name, Amen.

## ACTION STEP

Say "You can do it" to at least three students today, look them in the eyes when you do.

*When your voice says,*
*"You can," their fears begin to lose power.*

# REFLECTIONS

Write about the moments when you remind students, *you can do it.*

_____

_____

_____

_____

_____

_____

_____

_____

_____

_____

_____

_____

_____

_____

_____

_____

_____

_____

# DAY 41

# HELP

*"And the King shall answer... Inasmuch as ye have done it unto one of the least of these... ye have done it unto me."*
**(MATTHEW 25:40)**

## A TEACHABLE MOMENT

A student once asked me, "Will you help my cousin?" In that moment, I realized my role extended beyond my roster. When they trust me enough to bring someone they love into my care, whether for a need, a word, or a prayer, they've recognized God's light in me.

Your influence doesn't stop at the edge of your desk. It travels through families, communities, and generations, multiplying in ways you may never see this side of Heaven.

Teachers, when students share your name with others, they're sharing your light. Keep it shining.

Secretaries, you connect students not only to resources, but to each other. Your willingness to go the extra mile shows that your light makes the office a place of help, hope, and community.

## PRAYER

Heavenly Father, let my presence invite healing, not just for my students but for those they love, too. In Jesus' name, Amen.

## ACTION STEP

Be available today. Listen for the moments when a student wants to bring someone to your care or prayers.

*When they trust you with their people,*
*they trust you with their hearts.*

# REFLECTIONS

Reflect on how offering *help* extends God's love beyond the classroom.

_____

_____

_____

_____

_____

_____

_____

_____

_____

_____

_____

_____

_____

_____

_____

_____

_____

# SECTION 5

. . . . . . . . . . . . .

# INSTRUCTION
# &
# ASSESSMENT

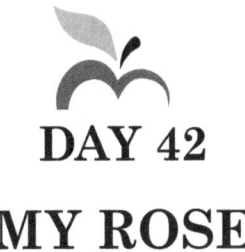

# DAY 42

# MY ROSE

## SCRIPTURE

*"I am the rose of Sharon, and the lily of the valleys."*
**(SONG OF SOLOMON 2:1)**

## A TEACHABLE MOMENT

Every classroom has roses, students with beauty, resilience, and potential hidden beneath layers of hardship or misunderstanding. Sometimes others only see the thorns, but a teacher's vision sees the bloom.

Growth is a process, and every student blooms differently. Some need more light, some need deeper roots, and some simply need time. As teachers, we are gardeners in God's field, nurturing each rose until it reveals its beauty. Teachers, your role is to provide light, nourishment, and time. Roses do not bloom overnight, and neither do students. Keep watering, keep speaking life, and watch God unfold the petals. Your patience today may be the sunlight that brings tomorrow's bloom.

Keep watering their potential with prayer. And when they bloom... You can whisper, *"Heavenly Father, there is your rose."*

## PRAYER

Heavenly Father, help me see beyond behavior into beauty. Teach me how to nurture each student in ways that align with Your timing until they bloom. In Jesus' name, Amen.

## ACTION STEP

Tell a student today what you see in them, something beyond the surface. Use your words to water a rose in hiding.

*Who needs to hear, "You're my rose?"*

## REFLECTIONS

Reflect on the hidden beauty of a *rose* in the classroom.

# DAY 43

# LESSON PLAN

## SCRIPTURE

*"For I know the thoughts that I think toward you, saith the Lord, thoughts of peace, and not of evil, to give you an expected end.*
**(JEREMIAH 29:11)**

## A TEACHABLE MOMENT

Some days, I feel like I have created the perfect lesson plan. Every activity is timed, and every standard is covered with relevance and clarity. But then, life happens. A student breaks down. A fire drill interrupts everything.

Or I just do not have the strength I thought I did. That is when God whispers, *"Follow My plan. Let Me Lead."*

If I begin the day with God, I will not be shaken when things do not go my way. The best classroom is one where I surrender the students, the lesson plan, and the pen and let Him write the day's story.

Teachers, you do not have to be perfect to be impactful. Sometimes the most powerful teaching moments come when we lay our plans at His feet and walk the path He sets before us. Stay present. Stay prayerful. Let Him take the lead.

## PRAYER

Heavenly Father, I release my plan to You today. Rewrite anything you need to lead me, guide me, and give me wisdom beyond the lesson plan. In Jesus' name, Amen.

## ACTION STEP

Before starting your day, pray over your lesson plan and ask God to make space for His will in your classroom.

*Always remember, God has already written your day. Trust the Author.*

# REFLECTIONS

Write about how God's hand guides your *lesson plan*.

_____

_____

_____

_____

_____

_____

_____

_____

_____

_____

_____

_____

_____

_____

_____

_____

_____

_____

_____

_____

# DAY 44

# THE BOARDS

## SCRIPTURE

*"Behold, I am doing a new thing...shall ye not know it?"*
**(ISAIAH 43:19)**

## A TEACHABLE MOMENT

I've watched the classroom evolve, chalkboards becoming Smart Boards, overhead projectors giving way to iPads, and textbooks shifting to digital screens. But while the tools have changed, the true heartbeat of teaching has not. The soul of education is still relationship, the power is still in truth, and the mission is still divine.

God placed me in *this* generation, and that means He's already equipped me to flourish in it. I am not intimidated by innovation; I'm inspired by it. Every new method is simply another channel for God's wisdom to flow.

Teachers, you were born for such a time as this. The shifts in education aren't just changes in technology; they're invitations for you to release fresh creativity, to pioneer new ways of reaching the heart, and to prove that while tools may evolve, the anointing remains timeless. You don't just adapt to change; you carry the anointing to lead through it.

## PRAYER

Heavenly Father, thank You. Technology may change, but Your voice, Your love, and Your presence in a student's life remain timeless. Equip me to teach in every season of change and with every tool. In Jesus' name, Amen

## ACTION STEP

Take 10 minutes today to learn one new teaching tool or tech trick, it might be the very thing that unlocks a student's potential.

*Adaptability is not a weakness; it's wisdom in action.*

# REFLECTIONS

Reflect on how teaching tools change, but truth remains beyond *the boards.*

# DAY 45

# NUMBERS

## SCRIPTURE

*"For where two or three are gathered in my
name, there am I in the midst of them."*
**(MATTHEW 18:20)**

## A TEACHABLE MOMENT

Some days, I see the roster and feel the weight of so many students, so many needs. But God reminds me: I'm not here to manage numbers; I'm here to minister to names. Every name belongs to a soul with a future Heaven cares about. Numbers may fill the attendance sheet, but God fills the assignment with purpose.

This isn't just a class roll, it's a list of divine appointments. Each student is a sacred trust, placed in my path for a reason only God fully knows. And if Heaven can number the hairs on their heads, I can surely see beyond their desks and into their destiny.

Teachers, never reduce your class to statistics. Each number has a name. Each name has a story. Each story has a God-written ending, and you've been entrusted with a chapter.

## PRAYER

Heavenly Father, give me strength to see beyond numbers and into hearts. Help me teach each one with care and calling. In Jesus' name, Amen

## ACTION STEP

Write the names of three students you'll intentionally speak life into today.

*Every number has a name. Every name has a purpose. Every purpose needs a teacher.*

# REFLECTIONS

Write about seeing beyond *numbers* to the names and stories they represent.

_____

_____

_____

_____

_____

_____

_____

_____

_____

_____

_____

_____

_____

_____

_____

_____

_____

# SECTION 6

## BEHAVIOR
### &
## RESTORATION

SECTION 8

# DAY 46

# AGAIN

## SCRIPTURE

*So then faith cometh by hearing, and
hearing by the word of God.*

**(ROMANS 10:17)**

## A TEACHABLE MOMENT

"Say it again," a student whispered. Not because they didn't
hear me, but because they needed to believe it. In that moment,
I realized repetition isn't just about comprehension, it's about
conviction.

Sometimes a student's heart has been told the opposite of the
truth so many times that it takes hearing the right thing again
and again before they can accept it.

Teachers, you hold the power to impart a truth deeper each
time we speak it. It may sound repetitive to us, but to them, it's
a lifeline slowly pulling them toward hope. Faith grows when

truth is repeated with love, whether it's academic encouragement, moral guidance, or words from the Word of God itself ... say it again.

## PRAYER

Heavenly Father, give me patience to speak life again and again until it takes root. Help me remember that some hearts need love on repeat. In Jesus' name, Amen.

## ACTION STEP

Repeat an encouraging truth to someone today until you see it in their eyes.

*Say it again because the second time hits the heart.*

# REFLECTIONS

Reflect on the power of speaking life *again* until hope takes root.

# DAY 47

# DISRUPTIONS

### SCRIPTURE

*"Thou wilt keep him in perfect peace, whose mind is stayed on thee: because he trusted in thee."*

**(ISAIAH 26:3)**

### A TEACHABLE MOMENT

There's always something. A student outburst. A technology glitch. A sudden schedule change. Disruptions will come but they don't have to control me.

Prayer helps me pause before I react. It anchors me in peace instead of panic. And when I invite Him in, God doesn't always remove the disruptions… but He gives me the wisdom to respond with grace. Every interruption becomes an invitation to return to the Source.

If you're navigating daily chaos, remember your peace is your power. When you lead from a posture of prayer, even the unexpected becomes an opportunity to display grace. You've got this... because God's got you. Rest in Him.

## PRAYER

Heavenly Father, when things shift suddenly, help me stay grounded in You. Let my peace be unshaken and my heart quick to pray, rather than panic. In Jesus' name, Amen.

## ACTION STEP

When a disruption happens today, take a deep breath and say: *"Heavenly Father, guide me."* Then respond.

*Peace is not the absence of noise. It's the presence of God in the middle of it.*

# REFLECTIONS

Write about how prayer steadies you in daily *disruptions*.

_____

_____

_____

_____

_____

_____

_____

_____

_____

_____

_____

_____

_____

_____

_____

_____

_____

_____

# DAY 48

# CONFLICT

## SCRIPTURE

*"Forbearing one another, and forgiving one another, if any man have a quarrel against any: even as Christ forgave you, so also do ye."*

**(COLOSSIANS 3:13)**

## A TEACHABLE MOMENT

Staff conflict can leave wounds that linger. Words spoken in stress. Misunderstandings that never got resolved. Silent tension that weighs down every meeting. But healing begins when I let go of the offense and lift up the name of Jesus. I have learned to bring those hard feelings to the One who understands betrayal and brokenness. He mends what I cannot fix and brings peace where pride once ruled. This isn't about winning arguments. It is about walking in freedom.

Teachers, healing begins when you surrender. Let go of the wounds and bring your hurts to Jesus, who understands and heals. It is not about being right but about finding peace and freedom in Him. With His help, you can walk in the freedom He offers, creating unity and reconciliation in every space you serve.

## PRAYER

Heavenly Father, I release the conflict I have been holding onto. Heal what is broken between us. Free my heart from bitterness and let me walk in the fullness of Your peace. In Jesus' name, Amen.

## ACTION STEP

Take a quiet moment to pray for the colleague you have struggled with most. Even if nothing changes outwardly, your heart will shift.

*Forgiveness is how you make space for God*
*to move in what you cannot control.*

# REFLECTIONS

Reflect on how forgiveness transforms *conflict* into peace.

# DAY 49

# I DON'T

## SCRIPTURE

*"Let your speech be always with grace, seasoned with salt..."*

**(COLOSSIANS 4:6)**

## A TEACHABLE MOMENT

Sometimes discipline comes wrapped in love. Saying, "I don't want to hear your name again," isn't rejection, it's a call to rise higher. I've heard it said before: "I don't want to hear your name again." But I've learned that correction without compassion wounds. The goal isn't to silence a child, it's to restore them.

Discipline that keeps dignity intact leaves a mark that builds, not breaks. Boundaries show them you care too much to let them self-destruct. Done with love, correction becomes direction.

Teacher, don't be afraid to speak the truth firmly. Students may resist in the moment, but later, they'll respect the guardrails you set.

## PRAYER

Heavenly Father, teach me to correct with love and speak with grace, even when I'm frustrated. Let my words heal while they guide. In Jesus' name, Amen.

## ACTION STEP

Reframe one correction today so it restores rather than shames.

*Correction is most powerful when wrapped in compassion.*

# REFLECTIONS

Write about restoring dignity, even when you must say, *I don't.*

_____

_____

_____

_____

_____

_____

_____

_____

_____

_____

_____

_____

_____

_____

_____

_____

_____

# DAY 50

# HOLD UP

## SCRIPTURE

*"Be still, and know that I am God..."*

### (PSALM 46:10)

## A TEACHABLE MOMENT

When chaos erupts, my first instinct used to be to react quickly. But I've learned the power of a holy pause, a moment to breathe, listen, and seek God's wisdom before moving forward.

This pause is not weakness; it's strength under control. It's giving the Holy Spirit the microphone before my emotions take the lead. In teaching, this kind of stillness can turn potential explosions into teachable moments.

Teachers, never underestimate the power of a pause, it can turn reaction into revelation.

Counselors: your quick thinking and slow presence keep students safe. Don't underestimate how your attention to detail speaks volumes about the value you place on every child in your care.

## PRAYER

Heavenly Father, help me to pause long enough to hear You. Teach me to respond, not just react. In Jesus' name, Amen.

## ACTION STEP

Practice a 10-second pause before correcting or confronting today. Let peace guide your tone.

*In the pause, God often gives perspective.*

# REFLECTIONS

Reflect on the strength of a holy pause; a moment to *hold up*.

# DAY 51

# SAY NO

## SCRIPTURE

*"But let your communication be, Yea, yea; Nay, nay: for whatsoever is more than these cometh of evil."*
**(MATTHEW 5:37)**

## A TEACHABLE MOMENT

Early in my career, I thought saying "yes" to every request was a sign of dedication. But I learned that overcommitment is a fast track to burnout. Sometimes the most loving word you can say is "no." Teachers often stretch themselves so thin serving everyone else that they leave nothing for their own rest and renewal.

Teachers, boundaries are not selfish they are essential. Saying "no" to what drains you allows you to say "yes" to what sustains you. Healthy boundaries protect your calling, preserve your energy, and keep your "yes" meaningful.

Protect your peace. Guard your purpose.

## PRAYER

Heavenly Father, give me wisdom to know when to say "yes" and courage to say "no" without guilt. Help me steward my time and energy in ways that honor You. In Jesus' name, Amen.

## ACTION STEP

Today, pause before saying "yes." Ask yourself: Is this aligned with my purpose, or just my pressure to please?

*Where in my teaching life have, I been saying "yes" when I should've said "no"?*

# REFLECTIONS

Write about the freedom and wisdom that comes when you *say no.*

_____

_____

_____

_____

_____

_____

_____

_____

_____

_____

_____

_____

_____

_____

_____

_____

_____

_____

# SECTION 7

· · · · · · · · · · · ·

RESILENCE
&
RENEWAL

# DAY 52

# WEIGHT

## SCRIPTURE

*"Come unto me, all ye that labour and are heavy laden, and I will give you rest."*

**(MATTHEW 11:28)**

## A TEACHABLE MOMENT

I do not always talk about it, but the weight of teaching is real. It is more than papers and meetings. It is the emotional load. The worry. The silent pressure to do enough… to *be* enough … to get it right.

But Jesus never asked me to carry it alone. I can lay it down: Every burden. Every worry. Every mistake. Every unspoken ache. He sees. He knows. And He is strong enough to carry me… carry you… carry our students and carry the calling.

So, if you are in a season of weariness, rest in this truth: You are not expected to be everything. You are not expected to do everything. You are not expected to get everything right. Just be faithful. Let God be your strength. The One who called you is also the One who will sustain you.

## PRAYER

Heavenly Father, I give You what is too heavy for me. The parts I cannot fix. The things I cannot say out loud. Be my strength. Be my rest. In Jesus' name, Amen.

## ACTION STEP

Write down one burden today. Tear it up as a symbol of giving it to God.

*You were never meant to carry it all. Lay it down. Breathe. Now get some rest.*

# REFLECTIONS

Now take a moment to lay down the *weight* you've been carrying and reflect on what God is lifting off of you.

---

---

---

---

---

---

---

---

---

---

---

---

---

---

---

---

---

---

# DAY 53

# INVISIBLE

## SCRIPTURE

*"Thou God seest me..."*

**(GENESIS 16:13)**

## A TEACHABLE MOMENT

Some days, I walk the halls, give my all, and still feel unseen. No one thanks me. No one asks how I'm doing. No one seems to notice. And yet I keep going.

But God sees. He sees when I show up in pain. He sees the late nights and the quiet tears. I am not invisible to Him. I am known. I am valued. I am appreciated. And so are you.

Teachers, even when no one claps, Heaven applauds— and that's enough. You are not invisible. Your presence carries purpose. Your voice, your faith, and your actions echo beyond the lesson plan. You are not just making it through the day, your presence is making a difference. Keep showing up.

## PRAYER

Heavenly Father, thank You for seeing me. When I feel over-looked, remind me that You're watching with love. Help me rest in Your validation, not man's. In Jesus' name, Amen.

## ACTION STEP

Write a note of appreciation to another teacher who may feel unseen. Be what you need.

*You are not hidden.*
*God sees your service and He smiles.*

# REFLECTIONS

As you pause, remind yourself, you are never *invisible* to God.
Reflect on where He has seen you clearly.

_____

_____

_____

_____

_____

_____

_____

_____

_____

_____

_____

_____

_____

_____

_____

_____

# DAY 54

# BURNOUT

## SCRIPTURE

*"He giveth power to the faint; and to them that
have no might he increaseth strength."*

**(ISAIAH 40:29)**

## A TEACHABLE MOMENT

Burnout does not always announce itself loudly. Sometimes,
it creeps in slowly through exhaustion, numbness, or apathy. I
used to think it meant I was weak. But now I know it means I
have been pouring from an empty cup. The truth is: I cannot
give what I do not have to give. So, I keep coming back to the
Source time and time again.

Prayer is not just how I begin the day, it is how to survive it.
God's strength never burns out. And when I lean into Him, I do
not just endure the day, I survive every challenge.

Teachers, when you feel the weight of burnout creeping in, remember you are not meant to do this alone. Return to the Source who never runs dry. Prayer refills your spirit and gives you the strength to rise above weariness. With God's strength, you will not just make it through the day you will end the day feeling renewed.

## PRAYER

Heavenly Father, breathe new life into my spirit. I am tired in ways only You understand. Be my strength. Restore my joy. Help me to serve with energy that comes from You. In Jesus' name, Amen.

## ACTION STEP

Choose one thing today to *release* from your plate. Say no to the extra so you can say yes to your health.

*You were not called to run on fumes.*
*Refuel. Re-center. Rest.*

# REFLECTIONS

Use this time to breathe and release every sign of *burnout* into God's renewing hands.

_____

_____

_____

_____

_____

_____

_____

_____

_____

_____

_____

_____

_____

_____

_____

# DAY 55

# RESTING

## SCRIPTURE

*"And he said unto them, Come ye yourselves apart into a desert place, and rest a while:"*

**(MARK 6:31)**

## A TEACHABLE MOMENT

Rest is not laziness. It is obedience. Jesus told His disciples to withdraw and rest. He knew that pouring out without refilling would leave them depleted. Yet, I often feel guilty for taking a break, saying no, or closing my door to breathe. But rest is sacred. When I embrace it, I model balance for my students and colleagues, too. I have learned that I am not more accurate because I hustle. I am more effective when I am whole.

Teachers, rest is a divine rhythm, not a sign of weakness. When you take time to recharge, you show your students and colleagues that balance is key to lasting impact. Embrace rest without guilt, knowing that God's strength flows through you when you are whole. You are more effective in His service when you care for yourself as He cares for you.

## PRAYER

Heavenly Father, teach me to rest without shame. Help me guard my boundaries with wisdom and live in the rhythm of grace, not constant hustle. In Jesus' name, Amen.

## ACTION STEP

Schedule one intentional rest moment this week: a walk, a nap, a quiet lunch alone. Honor it like it's sacred because it is.

*You do not have to earn rest. You are worthy of it, simply because you are His.*

# REFLECTIONS

Take these moments to lean into *resting* and write down how God is calling you to pause.

_____

_____

_____

_____

_____

_____

_____

_____

_____

_____

_____

_____

_____

_____

_____

_____

_____

# DAY 56

# IMPACT

*"Your labor is not in vain in the Lord."*
**(1 CORINTHIANS 15:58)**

## A TEACHABLE MOMENT

Some days you may wonder if your efforts matter at all, if you're simply repeating yourself, fighting battles you didn't start, and pouring out more than you feel you have. You long for your students to value what you pour into them, but sometimes it seems they don't. Yet God whispers a different truth: nothing done in love is ever wasted.

He notices every quiet act of kindness, every patient explanation, every prayer you lift. While the world often judges impact by immediate results, God measures by faithfulness and obedience. Your influence may not be visible today, but its effects ripple into eternity.

Teachers don't doubt your significance. Even on your hardest days, remember that because you choose to press on, lives are being changed. Your presence and hope are seeds God is using to transform families one at a time.

## PRAYER

Heavenly Father, remind me that what I do matters. Even when I do not see fruit, help me trust that You are growing something deep. Strengthen my faith to believe that my labor is never in vain. In Jesus' name, Amen.

## ACTION STEP

Reflect on one moment, a letter, a smile, a breakthrough that reminded you why you teach. Thank God for it.

*The fruit may grow in another season, but the seeds you planted today still count.*

# REFLECTIONS

Think about your *impact* beyond the classroom and note where you see God multiplying your efforts.

_____

_____

_____

_____

_____

_____

_____

_____

_____

_____

_____

_____

_____

_____

_____

_____

_____

_____

# DAY 57

# TEARS

## SCRIPTURE

*"Those who sow in tears shall reap in joy."*
**(PSALM 126:5)**

## A TEACHABLE MOMENT

I have taught through personal pain, smiling when I wanted to cry. But God sees every tear. And somehow, He turns pain into purpose. My tears are not wasted; they're watering the soil for someone else's breakthrough.

And in this post-pandemic classroom, where learning gaps are wide and weariness runs deep, I am reminded that what I carry matters. Every lesson taught in exhaustion, every prayer whispered over a struggling student, every moment I choose hope instead of giving up... it is all seen. God is still working through me, even when the results take time to show.

Teachers, keep going you are exactly the answer your students need, and your faithfulness today is shaping their tomorrow.

## PRAYER

Heavenly Father, thank You for seeing my silent tears. Use even my broken places to bring light and healing to me and my students. In Jesus' name, Amen.

## ACTION STEP

Close your eyes and give yourself permission to feel, but do not stop showing up. Speak life into what looks like a struggle.

*Tears do not mean you are weak. They mean you are human and still faithful.*

## REFLECTIONS

"Reflect on the gift of *tears* and what God is showing you through them."

_____

_____

_____

_____

_____

_____

_____

_____

_____

_____

_____

_____

_____

_____

_____

_____

# DAY 58

# JOY

## SCRIPTURE

*"Weeping may endure for a night, but
joy cometh in the morning."*

**(PSALM 30:5)**

## A TEACHABLE MOMENT

Certain seasons can leave us feeling depleted, as if the joy of teaching has slipped away. But take heart, joy isn't gone for good; it comes back when we allow ourselves rest, reflection, and renewal. God wants to give you joy again, not just survival.

He longs to fill you with genuine laughter and delight not just keeping your head above water but rejoicing in the small victories: a student's heartfelt thank-you note, a peaceful moment in a busy classroom, the simple triumph of another day's end. Joy is precious, and it is God who breathes it back into our souls.

So, hang on, dear teachers, joy is on its way. It is coming back. One day, one moment, one breath, and one blessing at a time.

## PRAYER

Heavenly Father, bring my joy back. Restoration, stress, and struggle have tried to steal my joy. Help me laugh again, love again, and teach again from a place of gladness. In Jesus' name, Amen.

## ACTION STEP

Do one thing that brings you joy today: music, nature, journaling, or dancing. Whatever awakens your spirit. Go for it.

*Joy does not always shout. Sometimes it returns quietly.*
*When it comes ... Welcome it back.*

# REFLECTIONS

Pause to name the places where *joy* is returning, even in small ways.

_____

_____

_____

_____

_____

_____

_____

_____

_____

_____

_____

_____

_____

_____

_____

_____

_____

# DAY 59

# IT HURTS

## SCRIPTURE

*"He healeth the broken in heart, and
bindeth up their wounds."*

**(PSALM 147:3)**

## A TEACHABLE MOMENT

Sometimes I walk into my classroom carrying my hurts, yet I
still show up. Other times, I see pain mirrored in a student's
silence, and we both feel it: it hurts. But I take heart in knowing
God draws near to the brokenhearted. Acknowledging my pain
doesn't weaken me; it reminds me I'm human.

I promise myself: I won't hide my scars, I'll let them guide
me. When I teach through my wounds with compassion, I
model genuine healing and give my students permission to grow
even as they learn. I have become living proof that God's power
shines brightest in my weakness.

Teachers, your courage to embrace pain and extend grace is a gift that transforms lives. Your presence, even on the hardest days, tells your students: it's okay to be real, and it's possible to find strength in the struggle.

## PRAYER

Heavenly Father, meet me and my students in the hurting places. Be our Healer and our hope. In Jesus' name, Amen

## ACTION STEP

Ask a student, "How are you really doing?" and listen carefully to what is not being said.

*It hurts but you are still here. That's strength.*

# REFLECTIONS

Take time to write honestly about where *it hurts* and how God is meeting you there.

_____

_____

_____

_____

_____

_____

_____

_____

_____

_____

_____

_____

_____

_____

_____

_____

_____

# DAY 60

# GIVING UP

### SCRIPTURE

*"He which hath begun a good work in you will perform it until the day of Jesus Christ."*

**(PHILIPPIANS 1:6)**

### A TEACHABLE MOMENT

Some students push every limit, but perseverance is a love language they understand. "Giving up on you is not an option." isn't just something I say it's something I live. When others walk away, I stay.

My endurance becomes their evidence that love can last. I show up even when progress is slow. I extend grace even when frustration is high. Because God never gave up on me, I cannot give up on them.

Teachers, your consistency is healing in action. Every day you stay is another day you show them they are worth the effort, worth the time, and worth the fight. Your presence speaks louder than any lecture; they may forget the words, but they will remember that you stayed.

## PRAYER

Heavenly Father, give me the strength to love like You, to never give up on the one's others would dismiss. Every day, give me the ability to declare by my actions that, *"You're worth it."* In Jesus' name, Amen.

## ACTION STEP

Reach out to a struggling student and an academically gifted student with a fresh start and fresh mercy today.

*"When others walk away, you stay. That's what makes you a teacher.*

# REFLECTIONS

Reflect on why you chose not to quit, and let the phrase *'giving up is not an option'* strengthen your spirit.

# DAY 61

# TEARS

## SCRIPTURE

*"Jesus wept."*

**(JOHN 11:35)**

## A TEACHABLE MOMENT

I used to think tears were a sign of weakness but in the classroom, they've become a source of strength. Every tear I've cried for my students has softened my heart instead of hardening it. Those tears have kept me compassionate when frustration tried to take over, patient when weariness wanted to win, and hopeful when outcomes seemed uncertain.

Tears remind me that I am not just teaching minds I am shepherding hearts. My tenderness keeps me from becoming mechanical in my work and keeps the classroom human in a world that can feel cold.

Teachers, your tears are not wasted. God bottles them, blesses them, and uses them to water the seeds you plant. The same heart that feels deeply will teach powerfully.

## PRAYER

Heavenly Father, thank You for sharing in my tears and shaping my heart to be tender like Yours. Let me never lose the ability to feel deeply, love fully, and serve faithfully. In Jesus' name, Amen.

## ACTION STEP

Turn your next moment of emotion into a prayer of intercession for your students.

*Tender hearts reach deeper than strong words ever could.*

# REFLECTIONS

Take time to reflect on how your *tears* have watered seeds of growth, both in you and your students.

_____

_____

_____

_____

_____

_____

_____

_____

_____

_____

_____

_____

_____

_____

_____

_____

_____

_____

# DAY 62

# FAILURE

## SCRIPTURE

*"Rejoice not against me, O mine enemy:*
*when I fall, I shall arise..."*

**(MICAH 7:8)**

## A TEACHABLE MOMENT

Failure isn't the end, it's part of the journey. I remind my students, "Failure is not final unless you stop trying." When we normalize struggle and model resilience, we teach them that falling down is only temporary. In God's hands, even failure becomes the foundation for growth.

Failure is not the end, it's a teacher of its own. I've seen students crumble under the weight of a bad grade, a poor choice, or a missed opportunity. My role is to remind them: this is a moment, not a life sentence.

When I help them see failure as feedback, they stop fearing it and start learning from it. The setback becomes a steppingstone.

Teachers, you are often the voice that rescues them from quitting. Keep reminding them that God uses all things, even failure, to shape us. The test they failed may be the very thing that teaches them resilience.

## PRAYER

Heavenly Father, give me the grace to rise every time I fall and to show my students that mistakes do not define their value. Let my testimony of resilience become their hope. In Jesus' name, Amen.

## ACTION STEP

Share a time when you failed and kept going, make it part of your testimony. "Falling doesn't define you, getting up does.

*Failure is a comma, not a period.*

# REFLECTIONS

Reflect on a *failure* that taught you resilience and how God used it for your growth.

# DAY 63

# I CAN

## SCRIPTURE

*"I can do all things through Christ which strengthened me."*
**(PHILIPPIANS 4:13)**

## A TEACHABLE MOMENT

Many students arrive convinced they can't. I love watching the shift from "I can't" to "Yes, I can." Sometimes it takes weeks, sometimes months, but the moment they say, "Yes, I can," something shifts.

That shift happens because someone believed in them long enough for them to believe in themselves. It's not just about academics; it's about mindset, resilience, and faith.

Teachers, every time you say, "Yes, you can," you are dismantling lies and building truth. That small declaration plants the seed of possibility and with God's strength, that seed can grow into destiny. Keep saying it until they can say it without you.

## PRAYER

Heavenly Father, help me remind every child that "Yes, I can" is rooted in You. In Jesus' name, Amen

## ACTION STEP

Have students say "Yes, I can" aloud—together. Then back it with action.

*Changing their words may change their world.*

## REFLECTIONS

Write out the places where God is turning 'I can't' into *I can* through His strength.

_____

_____

_____

_____

_____

_____

_____

_____

_____

_____

_____

_____

_____

_____

_____

_____

_____

# DAY 64

# STRENGTH

## SCRIPTURE

*"He maketh my feet like hinds' feet, and setteth me upon my high places."*

**(PSALM 18:33)**

## A TEACHABLE MOMENT

Some school years feel like mountain climbs. Progress is slow. Resistance is constant. But I've learned: God gives me the strength for every steep moment. Like a deer on rocky cliffs, I may not feel strong, but I'm equipped. I climb by grace, not by grit alone. Every lesson I teach on tough terrain matters.

Teachers, the height of your calling is revealed in the steepness of your climb. God is strengthening your steps. Every lesson, every moment of perseverance, is part of the climb toward something higher. Remember, God didn't just call you to the climb; He fitted your feet for it.

## PRAYER

Heavenly Father, steady my feet when I feel like slipping. Remind me that You've equipped me for every hill, every hallway, every heart I encounter. In Jesus' name, Amen.

## ACTION STEP

Take a five-minute prayer walk around your school and declare, "I have strength for this climb."

*When God calls you uphill, He strengthens every step*

# REFLECTIONS

Take a moment to reflect on where God has been your *strength* when you felt weak.

_____

_____

_____

_____

_____

_____

_____

_____

_____

_____

_____

_____

_____

_____

_____

_____

# DAY 65

# DON'T!

## SCRIPTURE

*Let us not be weary in well doing...*

**(GALATIANS 6:9)**

## A TEACHABLE MOMENT

When I was on the edge of quitting, my brother's words, *"Don't give up!"* reached through the storm --*"Remember why you started."* Those words became my anchor pulling me through nights of doubt and days of exhaustion. And here's the truth: my brother's voice still matters, but so does the united voice of every caring adult in a student's life.

When teachers, families, counselors, and staff join in that same chorus, we don't just encourage, we shift the atmosphere. We build a culture where perseverance is not the exception... it's the expectation.

Veterans, your "Don't give up" may be the last rope a student has left to cling to. Say it with conviction. Say it until hope rises in their eyes.

First-year teachers, there will be days when you'll wonder if you were meant for this. On those days, hear my brother's words in your spirit: *"Don't give up!"* Stand your ground. Be the steady, unwavering presence a student can count on.

Sometimes, one voice is enough to keep a dream alive. And when many voices speak together? That's when mountains move.

## PRAYER

Heavenly Father, give me the grace to keep going and to help others do the same. In Jesus' name, Amen

## ACTION STEP

Write "Don't give up" where you'll see it every morning.

*One voice of hope can silence a thousand reasons to quit.*

# REFLECTIONS

Think about the voices that told you '*don't* give up,' and reflect on the hope.

_____

_____

_____

_____

_____

_____

_____

_____

_____

_____

_____

_____

_____

_____

_____

_____

# DAY 66

# REBUILDING

## SCRIPTURE

*"And they said, Let us rise up and build. So they strengthened their hands for this good work."*

**(NEHEMIAH 2:18)**

## A TEACHABLE MOMENT

There are days when everything feels broken: test scores, behavior, and even morale. But like Nehemiah, I'm called to rebuild. Not with bricks and mortar, but with words and love ... with prayer, encouragement, and persistent teaching.

My classroom becomes a construction site of hope, and every prayer I whisper is a blueprint for restoration. God doesn't call me to fix it all, He calls me to rise and build with what I have.

Rebuilding doesn't happen in a day it happens in daily faithfulness. And while I'm restoring what's broken in my students, God is also rebuilding me.

Teachers, rebuilding in the classroom isn't about perfection; it's about persistent love and unshakable faith in what God can do through you.

Cafeteria workers, every act of rebuilding you do in your lunchroom is a declaration: "God is not finished here."

## PRAYER

Heavenly Father, give me the strength to rebuild what's been broken in my students, in my school, and in myself. In Jesus' name, Amen.

## ACTION STEP

Identify one "ruin" in your current situation. Begin praying and planning how to rebuild it with God as the Master Architect.

*You are not starting from scratch. You are starting from strength.*

# REFLECTIONS

Reflect on how *rebuilding* has shaped your relationship with your students.

_____

_____

_____

_____

_____

_____

_____

_____

_____

_____

_____

_____

_____

_____

_____

_____

_____

_____

# DAY 67

# DON'T LET

## SCRIPTURE

*"Wherefore I put thee in remembrance that thou stir up the gift of God, which is in thee..."*

**(2 TIMOTHY 1:6)**

## A TEACHABLE MOMENT

There's a subtle danger in teaching: getting so caught up in giving that you forget to keep growing. Busyness can quietly drain your passion until you're running on empty.

Burnout can happen quietly, one skipped break, one late night, one "I'll rest later," at a time. Before long, the passion you once carried feels buried under exhaustion. But you were not called to run on empty.

Teachers, you can't pour out effectively if you've stopped filling up. Stir your gift. Protect your joy. Make time to renew your spirit so you can show up whole, not hollow. I heard Him whisper, *"Don't let yourself go. You're more than this routine. You carry purpose. You carry light."* Custodians, I don't know where you are right now, but don't forget who you are. Stir up the gift. Light the fire again.

## PRAYER

Heavenly Father, breathe new life into me. Restore my joy and reignite my passion. Help me steward the gift You've placed in me. In Jesus' name, Amen.

## ACTION STEP

Take 15 minutes today to do something that restores you— pray, journal, walk, or rest. Guard the teacher within.

*What would it look like to take care of
the teacher God created in me?*

# REFLECTIONS

Don't let your fire go out; capture here what you need to keep it burning.

_____

_____

_____

_____

_____

_____

_____

_____

_____

_____

_____

_____

_____

_____

_____

_____

# SECTION 8

. . . . . . . . . . . .

PARTNERSHIP
&
COMMUNITY

# DAY 68

# PARTNERSHIP

## SCRIPTURE

*"Can two walk together, except they be agreed?"*
**(AMOS 3:3)**

## A TEACHABLE MOMENT

Parents and teachers, when we walk in unity, students flourish. But that partnership can be complex. Expectations clash. Communication fails. Emotions rise. That is why I pray first.

When I pray before the parent meeting, God softens hearts. When I pray for my family, the walls come down. We may not always agree, but we can always choose grace. Grace builds bridges that pride never could. When parents see Christ in me, it makes space for healing in them.

Teachers, your influence does not stop at the classroom door. You are not just shaping students; you are ministering to families. Every word you speak in love ... every moment you extend with grace … every action you give in kindness becomes a reflection of Christ. You may be the light that brings hope not only to a child, but to an entire home. Keep shining.

## PRAYER

Heavenly Father, help me be a partner, not a problem. Let my words be seasoned with wisdom and compassion. Help me see parents not as obstacles, but as allies in love. In Jesus' name, Amen.

## ACTION STEP

Pray over a difficult parent relationship today. Ask God to restore trust and build unity.

*When God leads the partnership, peace leads the process.*

## REFLECTIONS

Reflect on the power of *partnership* and how God is using you to build bridges.

_____

_____

_____

_____

_____

_____

_____

_____

_____

_____

_____

_____

_____

_____

_____

_____

# DAY 69

# BROKEN

### SCRIPTURE

*"He healeth the broken in heart, and
bindeth up their wounds."*

**(PSALM 147:3)**

### A TEACHABLE MOMENT

Some of my students carry wounds far too big for their age. They come from homes marked by tension, absence, or neglect. And while I cannot change their circumstances, I can lift them up in prayer.

When I see their pain, I do not turn away, I turn toward the throne. God hears the silent cries of children. He stands in the gap for single parents, grieving guardians, and fractured families. And when I intercede, I get to partner with Him in that healing work.

To the teachers who notice the hurt others overlook, your prayers are powerful. They are like seeds planted in tender hearts. You may not always see the harvest, but God is faithfully nurturing those seeds. Keep trusting the process. Your prayers are mending broken pieces that only Heaven can restore.

## A TEACHER'S PRAYER

Heavenly Father, cover the homes that are hurting. Be a father to the fatherless. Bring peace to homes full of chaos. Use me as a beacon of stability and hope in their lives. In Jesus' name, Amen.

## ACTION STEP

Choose one student and commit to praying daily over their family situation this week.

*You don't just manage space, you transform it.*

## REFLECTIONS

Take time to acknowledge the *broken* places you've seen and how God is bringing healing.

_____

_____

_____

_____

_____

_____

_____

_____

_____

_____

_____

_____

_____

_____

_____

_____

_____

# DAY 70

# BLAME

## SCRIPTURE

*"If it be possible, ...live peaceably with all men."*
**(ROMANS 12:18)**

## A TEACHABLE MOMENT

It is one of the hardest parts, being misunderstood and being blamed for what you did not do or what you could not control. As a teacher, I have been the target of frustration. Sometimes, when families are grieving or afraid, I become their outlet. But I have learned not to carry offense. I carry it to the cross.

God defends me when I stay humble. He fights for me when I stay faithful. I do not need to win every argument. I just need to walk in integrity.

To the teacher who feels misunderstood or misjudged, take heart. Your quiet obedience speaks louder in heaven than any earthly accusation. Stay steady. Stay humble. God is your defender, and your integrity is building a legacy no one can take away.

## PRAYER

Heavenly Father, help me not to take things personally. When I feel accused or misunderstood, help me respond with grace, not pride. Defend my heart and protect my peace. In Jesus' name, Amen.

## ACTION STEP

Forgive someone today; silently, sincerely. Let it go in prayer, even if you never hear "I'm sorry."

*Your calling is greater than their criticism.*
*Let God handle what you cannot.*

# REFLECTIONS

Pause to release any *blame* you have carried and reflect on the freedom forgiveness brings.

---

---

---

---

---

---

---

---

---

---

---

---

---

---

---

# DAY 71

# FAMILIES

### SCRIPTURE

*"Bear ye one another's burdens and
so fulfil the law of Christ."*

**(GALATIANS 6:2)**

### A TEACHABLE MOMENT

It is more than test scores and behavior charts. Sometimes, I become the person a family turns to when they have nowhere else to go, a phone call after hours, a tearful conversation in the parking lot, a grandparent just needing prayer.

In those moments, I know I am not just a teacher. I am a minister. This is not just my profession. It is my pulpit. So, I keep showing up, not because I am strong, but because He is.

And He keeps reminding me: *"When you serve them, you serve Me."*

Teachers, never forget the power of your presence. Every day you step into your classroom, you are more than just an educator, you are a vessel of God's love and grace. Your words, your actions, your compassion. They are shaping lives in ways you may never fully see. Keep trusting the process. It is working.

## A TEACHER'S PRAYER

Heavenly Father, thank You for the families You have entrusted to me. Let my service reflect your heart. Use every conversation, every act of compassion, to reveal your love. In Jesus' name, Amen.

## ACTION STEP

Reach out to a parent or guardian today just to encourage, not to correct or inform. Just to encourage their heart.

*The greatest ministry often looks like small moments of quiet faithfulness.*

# REFLECTIONS

Reflect on the *families* you've touched and how God is working through those connections.

_____

_____

_____

_____

_____

_____

_____

_____

_____

_____

_____

_____

_____

_____

_____

_____

_____

_____

# DAY 72

# UNITY

## SCRIPTURE

*"Behold, how good and how pleasant it is for brethren to dwell together in unity!"*

**(PSALM 133:1)**

## A TEACHABLE MOMENT

A unified team makes the whole school feel different. There is peace in the hallway, collaboration in meetings, and support when challenges rise. But unity does not happen by accident, it is built with prayer, humility, and grace.

I have learned to pray before I speak and forgive quickly when offended. Not every colleague will be easy to work with, but God can use me as a bridge where there has been a wall. We are stronger together. And when we invite Him in,

God becomes the glue that binds us in purpose, not just in profession.

Teachers, your willingness to extend grace and seek God's guidance creates a powerful spirit of unity. As you build bridges and forgive, His peace will flow through your school, strengthening every connection. With God at the center, you are stronger together. Keep trusting Him to work through you, both individually and as a team.

## PRAYER

Heavenly Father, help me walk in unity with my colleagues. Remove pride and replace it with peace. Help us work together in a spirit of harmony so that Your presence fills our school. In Jesus' name, Amen.

## ACTION STEP

Encourage a co-worker today. Send a message, leave a note, or offer to pray with them ... just because.

*Unity starts with humility. Let God use you to be the thread that weaves hearts together.*

## REFLECTIONS

Take a moment to write about where you've seen *unity* growing and where God is still calling you to sow peace.

_____

_____

_____

_____

_____

_____

_____

_____

_____

_____

_____

_____

_____

_____

_____

_____

_____

_____

# DAY 73

# BREAKROOM

## SCRIPTURE

*"Let your light so shine before men..."*
(MATTHEW 5:16)

## A TEACHABLE MOMENT

The breakroom can be a refuge or a battlefield. Some days it is filled with encouragement, other days with gossip or negativity. But what if you invited Jesus in first? When you carry His presence, you do not just react you lead. You become the thermostat, not the thermometer. A word of kindness, a choice to stay silent instead of slander, a prayer whispered under your breath; these small acts shift the atmosphere.

Teachers, you have the power to change a room just by showing up with Jesus. Let His light shine through you, even in the ordinary moments. Watch how hearts and environments begin to transform.

## PRAYER

Heavenly Father, help me bring Your presence into everyday spaces. Let my words be edifying, my spirit peaceful, and my influence gentle but strong. Shine through me. In Jesus' name, Amen.

## ACTION STEP

Today, speak one life-giving word in a shared space, and bless the atmosphere with encouragement.

*You do not have to preach. Just carry His presence.*
*That is enough to light up a room.*

# REFLECTIONS

Reflect on how you can carry God's light into ordinary spaces, even the *breakroom*.

_____

_____

_____

_____

_____

_____

_____

_____

_____

_____

_____

_____

_____

_____

# DAY 74

# MY MOTHER

## SCRIPTURE

*"Her children arise up, and call her blessed..."*
**(PROVERBS 31:28)**

## A TEACHABLE MOMENT

I stand on the shoulders of a woman who believed in me before I believed in myself. My mother Mary's faith was the soil where my confidence took root. She spoke into my potential when I could only see my mistakes. Teachers, you are often a "mother" in the faith to your students. Even when you're not related by blood, your words can birth courage in them. Your belief may be the spark that ignites their boldness.

When a student has a believing parent, it's a gift. But when school staff join that parent in belief, checking in, encouraging, and celebrating wins, it multiplies the impact. Teachers, belief grows when it's shared, and together we can keep the fire of confidence burning in students who might otherwise lose hope.

## PRAYER

Heavenly Father, help me believe in every child the way someone once believed in me. May my faith in them become the bridge they walk into their future. In Jesus' name, Amen.

## ACTION STEP

Tell one student today, "I believe in you," who doesn't yet see their worth.

*Belief may start at home but it grows in your classroom.*

## REFLECTIONS

Pause and write down the ways a *mother's* faith or encouragement has shaped who you are today.

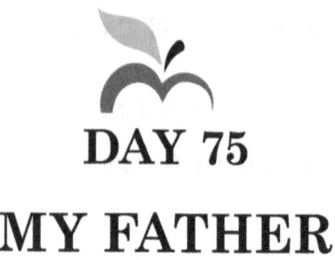

# DAY 75

# MY FATHER

## SCRIPTURE

*"I press toward the mark for the prize of the high calling of God in Christ Jesus."*

**(PHILIPPIANS 3:14)**

## A TEACHABLE MOMENT

My father James' push wasn't always comfortable, but it was purposeful. He saw more in me than I saw in myself. As a teacher, I've learned that pressure mixed with love becomes power.

I can still hear my father's voice, steady and sure, saying, "You may not get a second chance to make a first impression. Do it right the first time." He believed in doing things with excellence, not excuses. And when the finish line came into view, he'd remind me, "Always finish strong." But the words that still ring deepest are these: "Your name will go places you may never see. Be proud of who you are…." I knew what that meant … Be PROUD to be a KENT!

Those words built more than discipline; they built dignity. They made me carry myself with purpose, knowing that my actions didn't just reflect me, but the family and values I represent.

If you're just starting your teaching journey, know this: you may not yet see the impact, but every push you give toward excellence is shaping a life. Don't hold back because of inexperience; greatness is built one intentional nudge at a time. Veterans, continue to push with purpose. Greatness often begins where comfort ends.

## PRAYER

Heavenly Father, help me challenge and push my students with love so they can rise with strength and excellence." In Jesus' name, Amen

## ACTION STEP

Identify one student who needs a gentle push and speak to

*Greatness grows in the tension between pressure and purpose.*

# REFLECTIONS

Reflect on the lessons of strength and guidance that came through a *father's* voice or example.

# DAY 76

# BOUNDARIES

## SCRIPTURE

*"Iron sharpeneth iron..."*

**(PROVERBS 27:17)**

## A TEACHABLE MOMENT

My sister Sally loved me enough to say "no" when I wanted a "yes." Her boundaries weren't to restrict me but to protect me. Sometimes they came in the form of words of wisdom that made me pause. Other times, it was a certain look that spoke volumes without saying a word. And often, just her presence alone communicated to me that I needed to rethink my actions in the moment. Those boundaries left an imprint in my mind, an internal checkpoint I carried into my classroom and future moments of decision.

Boundaries in your classroom aren't barriers; they're bridges to learning. As first-year teachers, you may fear being too firm, but remember, clear, loving limits, create an atmosphere where students feel safe to grow. Boundaries are more powerful when they're consistent. They may resist now, but they'll thank you later for the guardrails that kept them on track.

## PRAYER

Heavenly Father, help me teach structures that nurture and free my students to grow and develop. In Jesus' name, Amen.

## ACTION STEP

Revisit one classroom rule and link it to a principle of purpose.

*Boundaries create the space where freedom can flourish.*

## REFLECTIONS

Consider how healthy *boundaries* protect both you and your students, and jot down where you need to set or honor them.

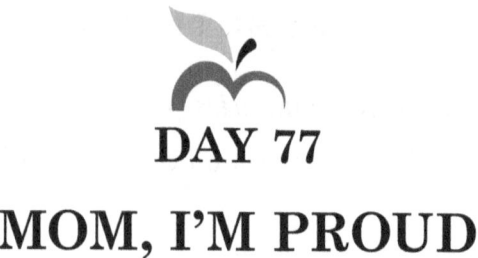

# DAY 77

# MOM, I'M PROUD

## SCRIPTURE

*"Her children arise up, and call her blessed..."*
**(PROVERBS 31:28)**

## A TEACHABLE MOMENT

When my daughter, Jas, spoke those words, I was reminded that my influence stretches far beyond the classroom. Our children, our students, our colleagues, even our administrators are all watching. They see us teach, serve, and persevere, and it speaks to their hearts: *Excellence is contagious.*

Veteran educators, your walk teaches the next generation how to lead with love and purpose. First-year teachers, one day a student will look at you with that same pride. Until then, show up with faithfulness and let your passion speak louder than your nerves.

Collaboration is more than sharing lesson plans; it's modeling a life worth following, on and off the clock. Your life is a lesson. Your consistency is the curriculum. And your love... is the legacy

## PRAYER

Heavenly Father, help me live in a way that inspires the ones I love and the ones I teach. "When they're proud of me I've already won." In Jesus' name, Amen

## ACTION STEP

Share a personal "I'm proud of you" moment with a student today.

*Your impact is bigger than your role.*

## REFLECTIONS

Take a moment to reflect on the voices, like *'Mom, I'm proud,'* that affirm your work and remind you why you keep going.

# SECTION 9

· · · · · · · · · · · · ·

MILESTONES
&
MOMENTS

# DAY 78

# WITNESS

## SCRIPTURE

*"The Lord hath done great things for us; whereof we are glad."*

**(PSALM 126:3)**

## A TEACHABLE MOMENT

Sometimes, I get to see it the turnaround. A parent starts showing up. A family finds stability. A child blossoms after months of prayer. It reminds me: Nothing is too hard for God.

Every answered prayer, every home restored is a miracle in motion. And I get a front-row seat. Not because I am perfect, but because I kept praying. God is always working behind the scenes.

Teachers, if you have been praying in silence, do not stop now. Your prayers are paving the way for transformation. Even when you cannot see it yet, God is moving. And when the breakthrough comes, you will know it was all worth it.

## PRAYER

Heavenly Father, thank You for healing families, restoring hearts, and answering prayers in ways only You can. Keep doing what only You can do for me. In Jesus' name, Amen.

## ACTION STEP

Celebrate one "miracle moment" today; write it down and thank God for letting you be part of the process.

*You are not just a witness. You are a warrior who prayed until something changed.*

# REFLECTIONS

Reflect on the moments you've been a *witness* to God's faithfulness in your classroom.

_____

_____

_____

_____

_____

_____

_____

_____

_____

_____

_____

_____

_____

_____

# DAY 79

# FINISH

## SCRIPTURE

*"I have fought a good fight, I have finished
my course, I have kept the faith."*

### (2 TIMOTHY 4:7)

## A TEACHABLE MOMENT

Finishing strong isn't about perfection or never making mistakes it's about faithfulness and perseverance. Some lessons may not have landed, some students may still be wrestling with the material, and even your best efforts might have felt insufficient. But God never called you to flawless performance; He called you to steadfast devotion.

Teachers, if you stayed the course, loved wholeheartedly, and showed up day after day, you have truly finished strong. Allow His grace to silence any doubt or guilt as you celebrate this milestone.

Congratulations Teachers! You haven't merely reached the finish line you've made a real difference. Be proud of every step you took and all you've accomplished.

## PRAYER

Heavenly Father, thank You for sustaining me. I give You every success and every struggle. Help me release what did not go as planned and celebrate what You have successfully done through me. In Jesus' name, Amen.

## ACTION STEP

Write a short note to yourself: "I am proud of you because…" Then read it aloud as many times as you need to affirm your accomplishment.

*You may be TIRED but you are STILL STANDING. And that alone is STRENGTH..*

## REFLECTIONS

Take time to celebrate how you've chosen to *finish* strong, even when the journey was tough.

_____

_____

_____

_____

_____

_____

_____

_____

_____

_____

_____

_____

_____

_____

_____

_____

_____

# DAY 80

# NEXT SEASON

## SCRIPTURE

*"To everything there is a season, and a time to every purpose under the heaven..."*

**(ECCLESIASTES 3:1)**

## A TEACHABLE MOMENT

Maybe one chapter is closing, and a new one is about to begin—and you don't have to face it with fear, because God is already there. He's the Author of your story and the One who orchestrates every transition. Even when change feels uncertain, His faithfulness never wavers.

The next season will not look like this one. If you look into the mirror, you will not look the same. And that is okay.

Because His plan is still good. His purpose is still unfolding. And you are still called, still equipped, and deeply beloved.

So don't be afraid to step forward. Step with courage, dear teachers. What awaits isn't just different, it's divinely appointed.

## PRAYER

Heavenly Father, I give You the unknown. Guide me into what is next with peace, clarity, and boldness. Thank You that every season, past, present, and future, is under Your care. In Jesus' name, Amen.

## ACTION STEP

Journal one prayer for your next season. Invite God to lead before you even take the first step.

*"Every ending is just God turning the page, your next season is already written in His faithfulness."*

# REFLECTIONS

Pause and reflect on the *next season* God is preparing you for with hope and expectation.

_____

_____

_____

_____

_____

_____

_____

_____

_____

_____

_____

_____

_____

_____

_____

_____

# DAY 81

# LETTING GO

## SCRIPTURE

*"He which hath begun a good work in you will perform it..."*
**(PHILIPPIANS 1:6)**

## A TEACHABLE MOMENT

Letting go is never easy, releasing the care you've poured into a student's life and trusting it will continue without you can feel impossible. But remember, you were never called to save them. You were called to be God's hands and feet for the season He entrusted them to you.

The same God who began a good work in your students will carry it to completion in their lives and in yours. As you release them, rest in the confidence that every seed you planted is safe in His loving care.

Breathe out the worry and breathe in His peace. You have given your best in faith and love, now watch how God brings the harvest. Trust this truth: faithful sowing always produces a bountiful return. Teachers, your labor is not in vain. Every word, every moment, every act of love matters more than you will ever know.

## PRAYER

Heavenly Father, I release every student, every plan, and every pressure to You. You are the finisher. I trust You to complete what I could only begin. In Jesus' name, Amen.

## ACTION STEP

Write the names of three students or families you are letting go of in prayer. Speak blessings over them as you release them now. You did your part. Now let God do His

*Change is not the enemy. It's often God's invitation into something new.*

## REFLECTIONS

Consider what God is asking you to release and write your reflections on *letting go*.

_____

_____

_____

_____

_____

_____

_____

_____

_____

_____

_____

_____

_____

_____

_____

_____

_____

# DAY 82

# FAITH

## SCRIPTURE

*"I have fought the good fight, I have finished
the race, I have kept the faith."*

**(2 TIMOTHY 4:7)**

## A TEACHABLE MOMENT

The year has tested me, but I'm still standing, not in my own strength but upheld by the grace of God. I didn't just survive, I showed up when it was hard, stayed faithful when it would've been easier to quit, and poured out my best even when I felt empty. What felt like pressure was actually God shaping me, stretching me, and producing purpose in ways I couldn't yet see.

Every lesson taught, every tear prayed over, every parent I met— all mattered. And the same God who carried me through this year will continue the good work in every life I've touched. My labor has not been in vain.

Teachers, take a deep breath and let this truth settle in: you didn't just make it through you made a difference. You are not leaving this year empty you are leaving it faithful, fruitful, and favored.

## PRAYER

Heavenly Father, thank You for carrying me through. Pour back into every space I poured out. "You stood. You served. You stayed faithful. That's victory." In Jesus' name, Amen

## ACTION STEP

Speak this over yourself: "I am finishing strong, by faith."

*Your finish matters just as much as your start.*

# REFLECTIONS

Reflect on the moments where *faith* carried you when strength alone wasn't enough.

_____

_____

_____

_____

_____

_____

_____

_____

_____

_____

_____

_____

_____

_____

_____

_____

_____

# DAY 83

# LESSONS

## SCRIPTURE

*"But lay up for yourselves treasures in heaven... For where your treasure is, there will your heart be also."*
**(MATTHEW 6:20–22)**

## A TEACHABLE MOMENT

One day, the lesson plans will be packed away, the walls will be bare, and the final bell will ring. But my impact will keep walking out of this room in the lives I've touched.

The world may measure my work in scores and statistics, but Heaven measures it in seeds planted, prayers prayed, and hearts transformed. That's why I teach—not for the applause of today, but for the harvest of tomorrow.

Teachers, your greatest work will outlast your career.

You are building something that time cannot erase: a legacy of truth and love that will echo in generations you may never meet.

## PRAYER

Heavenly Father, help me teach beyond the moment. Let my legacy be one of love, faith, and eternal impact. In Jesus' name, Amen

## ACTION STEP

Identify one way you've seen your influence outlive the lesson, write it down, and thank God for the reminder.

*The most powerful parts of your teaching will not show up in test score data.*

# REFLECTIONS

Take a moment to jot down the *lessons* you want to carry forward into the future.

_____

_____

_____

_____

_____

_____

_____

_____

_____

_____

_____

_____

_____

_____

_____

_____

_____

_____

# DAY 84

# BEYOND

## SCRIPTURE

*"And whatsoever ye do, do it heartily, as to the Lord, and not unto men."*

**(COLOSSIANS 3:23)**

## A TEACHABLE MOMENT

The bell may signal the end of a class, but it does not mark the end of my assignment. My influence lives beyond the ring of the bell, beyond the walls of my classroom, beyond the moment they pack their bags. Seeds planted in faith do not clock out; they continue to grow in the quiet spaces of a student's life.

Beyond the bell, my words replay in their minds when they face a decision. Beyond the bell, the example I set becomes a compass they carry. Beyond the bell, my prayers still cover them like a shield, even when I am not there to see the battles they face.

Teachers, your greatest work often happens in the unseen. What you plant in the light of day blooms in the hidden places of the night. You are not just teaching for today's lesson—you are shaping tomorrow's leaders, healers, innovators, and servants of God. The bell may end the period, but it cannot end your purpose.

## PRAYER

Heavenly Father, help me to see my classroom through eternal lenses. Let me never underestimate my impact. In Jesus' name, Amen

## ACTION STEP

Pray for your classroom today before and after the bell.

*Teaching with faith doesn't stop at the bell, it echoes into forever.*

# REFLECTIONS

Reflect on the ways your impact goes *beyond* the classroom and into eternity.

_____

_____

_____

_____

_____

_____

_____

_____

_____

_____

_____

_____

_____

_____

# DAY 85

# SUCCESS

### A TEACHABLE MOMENT

The day a struggling student finally gets it, the moment a once-resistant learner turns in work with pride, that's success. It may not be perfect, but it's progress. And I've learned to celebrate it out loud: "Welcome to success!"

Success is not just an achievement; it's a mindset. When I declare it over them, I'm giving them permission to see themselves differently. I'm telling them they belong in the space where victories happen.

Teachers, welcome your students into success as if it's a room they've always had a key to. When you celebrate their wins, you're teaching them that hard work is worth it and that they were always capable.

## PRAYER

Heavenly Father, let my words unlock dreams in my students. Teach me to celebrate progress as much as achievement, and to speak identity over them until they believe it for themselves. In Jesus' name, Amen.

## ACTION STEP

Tell a student today: "Welcome to success" and explain why you see it in them.

*Success starts with someone who believes they belong there.*

# REFLECTIONS

Pause to celebrate small wins and write about what *success* looks like in God's eyes. In your department.

_____

_____

_____

_____

_____

_____

_____

_____

_____

_____

_____

_____

_____

_____

_____

_____

# DAY 86

# FIRST GRADE

## SCRIPTURE

*"Before I formed thee in the belly I knew thee..."*
**(JEREMIAH 1:5)**

## A TEACHABLE MOMENT

My first-grade teacher saw something in me that I hadn't seen yet. She spoke it before I believed it. She called it out and watered it with encouragement. Thank you, Miss Ellis. Now I get to do the same for others.

Some teachers see potential early. When that insight is shared with counselors, parents, and future teachers, it becomes a roadmap that guides a child for years.

Teachers, the wisdom we share as a team can become the legacy that shapes a student's destiny long after they've left our classroom. You may be the first to recognize a gift in a student. Your affirmation could be the first confirmation they ever receive.

## PRAYER

Heavenly Father, help me see greatness in students before it fully shows. Someone saw it in me. Now help me pay it forward. In Jesus' name, Amen

## ACTION STEP

Affirm a student's gift today, even if it's just a spark.

*Great teachers don't just teach, they prophesy potential.*

# REFLECTIONS

Think back to those who first believed in you, like *first grade* teachers, and reflect on how you now carry that forward.

# DAY 87

# STORY

## SCRIPTURE

*"The Lord bless thee, and keep thee..."*
**(NUMBERS 6:24A)**

## A TEACHABLE MOMENT

Every year, you've poured out lessons, love, prayers, discipline, and encouragement. You've stood when it was easier to sit down. You've believed in students when others counted them out. Through it all, you have told the story of God's faithfulness without ever opening a Bible in class because your life has been the chapter they needed to read. Teachers, your story matters because it points to His story.

Don't just teach content, live a testimony. When students remember you, let them remember the steady voice that spoke truth, the presence that carried peace, and the heart that didn't give up. Part of your legacy is the testimony you carry. Athletic

Coaches, share your victories, your valleys, and the God who met you in both. Students and colleagues alike need to see that teaching is more than a profession, it is a God-ordained story of service and impact.

## PRAYER

Heavenly Father, thank You for the calling You've placed on my life. Restore what was depleted, refresh what was forgotten, and reward what was done in secret. Let my story be a living testimony of Your grace. In Jesus' name, Amen.

## ACTION STEP

Share one personal story of perseverance with your students or colleagues this week. Show them that success is possible, even when the journey is hard.

*You are God's beloved educator. Now,*
*He will take it from here.*

# REFLECTIONS

Write about how your *story* points to God's greater story of faithfulness.

_____

_____

_____

_____

_____

_____

_____

_____

_____

_____

_____

_____

_____

_____

_____

_____

# DAY 88

# I KNEW

## SCRIPTURE

*"My sheep hear my voice ..., and they follow me."*

**(JOHN 10:27)**

## A TEACHABLE MOMENT

There are moments when God highlights a student quietly, unmistakably. You may not know their full story, but you know you are meant to speak life into them. Those nudges are divine appointments.

God will sometimes highlight a student to you in the middle of your busy day. It may not make sense in the moment, but that gentle nudge to encourage, pray for, or check on them could be life changing.

Teachers, when you follow that still, small voice, you step into God's perfect timing for a life you may never fully know you've changed. Don't ignore the still, small voice. Your words in that moment may be the lifeline that shifts a student's entire trajectory. Never underestimate the power of one Spirit-led sentence.

## PRAYER

Heavenly Father, help me hear Your voice clearly and respond quickly when You nudge me toward a student. In Jesus' name, Amen.

## ACTION STEP

Ask the Holy Spirit to highlight one student today. Pray for them. Speak life over them. Let them know they are seen.

*Have I ever felt the nudge to speak
encouragement but ignored it?*

# REFLECTIONS

Reflect on the times you *knew* God was nudging you toward a student, a decision, or a word of encouragement.

_____

_____

_____

_____

_____

_____

_____

_____

_____

_____

_____

_____

_____

_____

_____

_____

_____

# DAY 89

# I FORGAVE

### SCRIPTURE

*"And be ye kind one to another,
tenderhearted, forgiving one another..."*
**(EPHESIANS 4:32, KJV)**

### A TEACHABLE MOMENT

There were moments I could've stayed offended when a student rolled their eyes, when a parent misunderstood me. I had every reason to carry it, but I made a different choice: "I forgave you when it happened." Not because it didn't hurt, but because I refuse to let bitterness block the flow of grace in my life.

Forgiveness isn't weakness, it's wisdom. It keeps my heart clear so I can keep showing up with compassion, clarity, and Christ.

Teachers, forgiveness is a gift not just to others, but to yourself. When you let go, you make room for love to lead again.

Your classroom becomes lighter. Your words gain weight. And your heart stays whole.

## PRAYER

Heavenly Father, help me forgive quickly, sincerely, and fully. Keep my spirit tender and my heart open so Your healing can flow through me. Amen.

## ACTION STEP

Ask God to reveal any lingering offense. Speak out loud: "I forgave you when it happened"

*Forgiveness isn't about forgetting; it's about freeing your heart to keep loving.*

## REFLECTIONS

Take time to write about the freedom you've found when you forgave from a pure place.

_____

_____

_____

_____

_____

_____

_____

_____

_____

_____

_____

_____

_____

_____

_____

# DAY 90

# BENEDICTION

## SCRIPTURE

*"The Lord bless thee, and keep thee..."*

**(NUMBERS 6:24A)**

## A TEACHABLE MOMENT

The year has been full of challenges, victories, and everything in between. You've poured out of yourself for your students, your school, and your community. And now, God invites you to rest, not because the work isn't important, but because you are.

You have given your best; your time, energy, wisdom, and heart. Now again, God invites you to rest. This is not an ending; it is a pause before the next chapter.

Teachers, receive His blessing over your life, your work, and your future. You have planted faithfully, and heaven has recorded every seed. The God who called you is the God who will carry you into your next assignment. You are a CHAMPION.

Principals may joy return like morning light, and may grace go before you into every new assignment. You have led well. You have monitored carefully. Now rest boldly I CHAMPION YOU.

## PRAYER

Heavenly Father, thank You for the privilege of teaching. Bless me with deep rest and renewed strength for the days ahead. In Jesus' name, Amen.

## ACTION STEP

Take time this week to celebrate what God has done through you this year.

*You are God's beloved educator. Now,*
*He will take it from here.*

# REFLECTIONS

Use this space to reflect on the *benediction* over your year, God's blessing, His covering, and His peace for what comes next.

# BLESSINGS & REFLECTIONS

You made it to the final page—but this is not the end. It is a new beginning. This journey was never about perfection. It was about presence—God's presence in your classroom, your calling, and your everyday moments of obedience.

As you move forward, may you:

- Continue to invite Him in, even when the room is loud or your spirit feels weary.
- Carry the confidence that your work matters, even when no one says it.
- Speak life over your students, your colleagues, and yourself.
- Teach with eternity in mind, knowing your reward is in Heaven.

Let this devotional be a reminder that you are called, you are covered, and you are never alone.

*You are loved.*
*You are seen.*
*You are chosen.*
*And the best is yet to come.*

You can find this paperback and ebook at www.amazon.com under my name and title.
To connect, learn, or explore future devotionals and workshops, visit www.thehouseoflomax.com.

Made in the USA
Columbia, SC
14 January 2026

77988273R00173